INDIA

© 2006 Rebo International b.v., Lisse, The Netherlands

Text and Photography: Günter Heil
Cover Design: AdAm Studio, Prague, The Czech Republic
Lay-out: AdAm Studio, Prague, The Czech Republic
Typesetting: AdAm Studio, Prague, The Czech Republic
Translation: Abandon Agency, Prague, The Czech Republic
Proofreading: Sarah Dunham

ISBN 13: 978-90-366-1898-4
ISBN 10: 90-366-1898-3

INDIA

Photography and text: Günter Heil

REBO
PUBLISHERS

Contents

Topics

Traveling through India

Topics

The Country – a Continent!

The area along the coast between Kochi and Kollam is called Kuttanad. This land is filled with lagoons and canals. Roads here are often waterways: the famous backwaters.

9

The Country – a Continent!

India is the sixth largest country in the world. The distance between the northern border on the roof of the world and Kanyakumari at the most southern point of the subcontinent is 1,997 miles. The distance between the border with Burma in the east and with Pakistan in the west is 1,822 miles. This enormous area is divided into several imposing landscapes. One billion people live in this country. They differ greatly in origin, appearances, religion, customs and habits. Over the course of their long and turbulent history, Indians have produced a prismatic and dynamic culture while suffering surprisingly often from natural disasters, war and intolerance.

On the other side of the backbone of the Himalaya is the river oasis of Ladakh, located in a grandiose desert landscape. The Himalaya Front Range is the valley landscape of Kashmir. The Chenab, Ravi, Beas and Sutlej river valleys, with their impressive terrace cultures, temples and palaces, have long since disappeared.

Punjab is located in the western part of the large North Indian low-lying plains, the fertile land of five rivers. It is the homeland of the Sikhs and one of India's granaries. This area is bordered to the south by the dry, grassy plains of Rajasthan. The Aravalli hills divide the arid land from the 'green' Rajasthan, which benefits from the monsoons. The enormous, low-lying plains of the Ganges pan out east of Delhi. The river and its tributaries form the distinctive *Doabs*, which make up the agriculturally vital land from two streams. The Ganges and the Brahmaputra Rivers join again in Bangladesh, where they form an

enormous delta at the Gulf of Bengal. These North Indian plains, which cover around a quarter of the land mass and include the centers Delhi and Patna, were culturally significant from mythical times as the mainland of mighty empires and the base for conquering distant regions.

The Dekan peninsula was part of the ancient continent known as Gondwana. The mountainous and forested north between Gujarat and West Bengal – known as the *tribal belt* – is inhabited by half of all *adivasis* (tribal members) of India. The actual Deccan plateau is surrounded by mountains and steepens sharply in the east. The river streams that spring from the Western Ghats flow through the imposing granite landscapes in the east and pass into the Gulf of Bengal. Muslim sultanates battled here with the last Hindu Empire, Vijayanagar. The imposing relics of these cultures provide the stony plains with even more charm. The Nilgiri and Cardamom Mountain Ranges form the Anaimudi, the highest point in South India at 8,842 feet. In the south-west, the central Deccan mass is bordered by the tropical Malabar Coast which flows into the old cultural landscape of Konkan. Along the east coast of the subcontinent, the ancient Coromandel Coast stretches to where ships from the ninth and tenth centuries exported India's culture to the east and southeast.

A cultured landscape east of Ladakh. Mostly barley and potatoes flourish at this altitude, but only in areas where the cultivated land can be irrigated with icy water from the streams. The cultivated land at the Chemre monastery is located in a somewhat sloping area and is supported by walls of stacked rocks.

At 18,392 feet, Khardung La in Ladakh is the highest mountain pass in the world.
This road connects the valley of the Indus with the Nubra. The 20,000 foot high mountains
of the Ladakh range can be seen from this mountain pass.

The valleys of the tributaries of the Indus in the Himalaya Front Range are ancient landscapes. The lovely terraces of the mountain paddy fields stretch far up the slopes to the upper stream of the Ravi.

Ladakh is located on the side of the main ridge of the Himalaya, where the monsoon rains rarely reach. Where irrigation is not possible, the landscape is a dry, rocky desert surrounded by snow-covered mountains and decorated with stupas, which are religious symbols of the pious Ladakhis.

The folds on the main back of the Himalaya sediments are transported to lonely heights at the Lamayuru monastery in Ladakh. Here they have gradually disintegrated to create a bizarre, moon-like landscape.

Landscapes with quarries to the east of Nagaur.
Brilliant sculptures on the houses
and on the palaces of this country are carved
out of the sandstone.

In the west, Rajasthan mostly consists of dry
fields which extend into the Thar Desert.
The residents of this region meet once a year
at Ajmer for the great Pushkar Mela.

The 'green' Rajasthan starts from the east of the
Aravalli Mountains. The monsoons create great
water reservoirs, such as the one pictured,
north of the Bundi.

Facing the Meherangarh Fort in Jodhpur, the capital city of the Marwar region. The blue gleam comes from the numerous electric-blue painted houses of the Brahmans in Jodhpur.

Chili harvest in Rajasthan. These sharp chilies are dried outside after the harvest and before they are finely ground into the indispensable chili powder of Indian kitchens.

At Osian, an old temple city North of Jodhpur, the dry fields abut a desert landscape with high sand dunes.

The Jain temples of Ranakpur are hidden in a valley in the southern Aravalli Mountains. The open forests vibrate with a lovely, fresh green during the monsoon period.

The rulers of Vijayanagar established their capital city on the Deccan plateau in a brilliant landscape, characterized by granite mountains along the river at Tungabhadra. The Virupaksha temple, which is highly revered, survived the destruction of the parent state and currently forms the center of the humble town of Hampi.

Fertile soil abounds in the slopes around Vijayanagar. Blossoming sugar cane provides the landscape with unique charm during November and December.

As if placed there by a giant hand, large granite rocks lie on top of each other, weathered by the wind and water. Every now and then, modest relics of old buildings, made from the same material, can be seen in among them.

The tree that is the most typical for these stony plains of Tamil Nadu is the tall, slim Palmyra palm, typically found in clusters.

In the higher elevations of the mountains between Kerala and Tamil Nadu, the landscape is defined by round, dark green cushions of tea bushes: a monoculture that is ever present at a certain height and just as quickly interchanged with different cultures.

Palms, women on the paddy fields and a pond with lotuses against the blue mountains: a typical image of the fertile plains of Tamil Nadu.

During the second harvest in Karnataka, not far from the coast, farmers plow together; the rice is sowed by hand.

Young rice plants are harvested and replanted in neat rows during the northeast monsoon in the Cauvery delta in Tamil Nadu.

Deep green paddy fields at the foot of the Palni Mountains in Tamil Nadu.

Spread over a park-like landscape at Gwalior in Madhya Pradesh are the palaces and temples of the rulers of Scindia.

The naked mountain ridge looks magical with a few lonely old temples and the secret round temple for the 64 yoginis.

The landscape at the foot of the Golkonda is meager and stony. Only the tombstones of the Qutb Shahi rulers crowned with domes are in well-maintained gardens.

In the tropical coastal area of Kerala, water and land converge. Fresh green vegetation abounds.

Red laterite stones rise up along the beach at the coast at Varkala in southern Kerala. For many centuries, this place, with its ancient temples was a destination of Hindu pilgrimages. Now it has been discovered by international world travellers.

The lagoons and lakes of Kuttanad give people food and work. Processing sand for the building industry and fishing are very important economically.

Religion and society

During the era of Indira Gandhi, the town youth of Alampur made an appeal to its people to limit the birthrate. These educational campaigns have had a positive effect especially among the middle classes, though the population is still growing rapidly.

Religion and society

The official religion of the Indian people is Hinduism. 83 percent of the population consider themselves practicing Hindus. The word 'Hindu' is derived from 'Indus,' the life vein of early India, referred to by its neighbors as Hindustan. Hinduism is the result of thousands of years of development, the smelting of different religions and cults as well as the integration of foreign gods and opposing ideas. It can, therefore, be referred to as a 'collective religion.' In modern Hinduism, the innumerable gods are interpreted as aspects and shapes of the divine trinity Brahma – Vishnu – Shiva, equated in turn with the universal spirit, Brahma. In this way, enlightened Indians interpret Hinduism as a monotheistic religion.

Hinduism is not only a religion, however. It is also a moral philosophy, a way of life and a social order to which everyone is assigned a place at birth. Social and ethical behavior affect how an individual will be reincarnated. The basis of the social order consists of multiple levels in a caste system.

Blanket division on the basis of *varna* (color) dates back to the time when Aryans established the system of holding back indigenous inhabitants with skin colors darker than their own. The division is hierarchic: *Brahmanas* (priests), *kshatriyas* (warriors), *vaishyas* (farmers) and *shudras* (servants). Outside the hierarchy are the *dalits* (the 'untouchables') and the *adivasis* (tribe members). More importatnt for the individual and society is the division of the countless jatis (*jati* means birth). These groups can be subdivided by means of the most obvious criteria, such as ethnic background, cultural tradition, religion and occupation. With economical development, new jatis are added to the mix. Perhaps dabawallahs? Or lumberjacks? Jatis are divided into hierarchies, depending on their supposed levels of purity. The one thing they have in common is that they are only allowed to marry within their group.

Eleven point four percent of the population practices Islam. Despite the fact that one of the most prominent principals of Islam is equality, its social system can be compared to the caste divisions of the Hindus. There is actually not a single religious community in India that significantly distances itself from the caste system. Among Christians, who make up 2.4 percent of the population, a caste hierarchy is present. The Sikhs make up 2 percent, Buddhists 0.7 percent and Jains 0.5 percent of the population.

The great variety of religions practiced in India has brought about a culture of tolerance over the centuries. People used to live together in peace and often celebrated their festivals together. However, with modern nationalism, religious fundamentalism and political abuse, this tolerance is sadly vanishing.

At the top of the 2,600 foot Pavagadh Mountain
and visible from afar is the strongest fortress
of Gujarat, a frequently visited temple
of the mother goddess, Bhavani Devi.
A shrine to the honor of Sadan Shah,
a Muslim holy, rests on the broken towers.

After conquering Daulatabad in 1318, the
Sultan of Delhi had the first complex of the
Great Mosque built on the same location with
material from the demolished Jain and Hindu
temples. There is currently a statue of worship
in the prayer area of the mosque of the Hindu
mother goddess who is revered as Bharatmata,
'Mother of India.'

Dattatreya is Brahma, Vishnu and Shiva rolled into one. He is represented over and over again on a stone pillar on the *ghats* (fields next to the river) of Varanasi by two symbols of the three gods in his six hands.

The groups of figures depicted on one of the gate towers of the Minakshi temple in Madurai shows Shiva triumphing over Narasimha and Vishnu, incarnated as the terrifying monster, Sarabha.

Aiyanar transformed himself from a protecting Tamil god into an idol of an enormous community of young, active followers who united once again the worshippers of Shiva and Vishnu. This brightly lit shrine has been placed on a truck.

The motif of the lion-elephant can often be seen in temples, such as on the Vital Deul in Bhubaneshwar here. It symbolizes the predominance of Hinduism over Buddhism.

Small shrines in the streets of the cities offer their visitors food for meditation. The selection is broad: Shiva, Krishna, Rama and, of course, Hanuman and Ganesha.

The *mihrab* (prayer niche) of the Great Mosque of Bijapur reflects the power and artistry of the Adil-Shahi sultans and asserts the power of Islam.

Muslims devote themselves to prayer and religious discussion in a mosque of Ajmer's Holy Shrine.

Muslims listen to a sermon of an Imam in the Bazaar of Bhopal.

A religious Muslim studies the Koran in the courtyard of the *dargah* (mausoleum) of Khwaja Muin-ud-din Chishti.

A group of young *qawwali* musicians sing songs professing their love of God in front of the gravestone of the holy.

Christian Indians do not form a cohesive
'Christian community,' but are actually much
divided over religious issues.
The so-called St Thomas Christians of Kerala,
for example, whose community has been in
existence since pre-colonial days, have split
into fifteen 'churches.' Followers of the patriarch
fraction of the Malankara church celebrate the
visit of the patriarch on the 'Day of
the Patriarch' with colorful processions.

Oriental elements can be clearly seen within the Syrian Christian traditions while members of English mission churches embrace Western traditions, including apparel, such as with this bride and her entourage in Madras.

The Christians in Kerala try to connect with the traditions of Hinduism in their holy places. Thus beautiful bronze flagpoles stand in front of some churches, as are normally found at Hindu temples. Instead of the *lokapalas* – the world watchers of the eight wind directions – on the dado, there is Christ on the cross and various other religious reproductions.

In Ajmer in the 1820s, a devout diamond dealer depicted the cosmology of the Jains and the life of Rishabha, the first of the 24 *tirthankara's* (prophets), in an enormous mirrored room. In Soniji ki Nachiya, the visitor can see how the concentric world is arranged around Meru Mountain. 'Airships' fly with heavenly musicians. This brilliant work, containing one ton (two thousand pounds) of gold, can be seen from three galleries from every angle.

Bahubali was the son of Rishabha. In Sravana Belgola, the center of the Jain following of the *digambaras* ('clothed in the quarters of the sky'), is a granite image 57.4 feet high.

The stone pillar of the well with the stairs of the queen of Patan names Buddha the ninth incarnation of Vishnu. This integration of Buddha in Vishnuism came forth from the efforts of orthodox Brahmans to establish the primacy of their own religion over Buddhist doctrine.

The great Indian, Tantricus Padmasambhava, came to Ladakh in the eight century and ensured the blossoming of Hinduism. At miracle plays, such as here in the Hemis monastery, with the use of various masks, he is portrayed as a highly placed lama.

The religion of the Sikhs dates back to Guru Nanak at the beginning of the sixteenth century when Hinduism was striving to renew itself and the ethnic basis of Sikhism was defined. The pacifist community later converted into a warlike order under the influence of the Mogul emperors. The Nihangs and their customs are remnants of this heroic time.

Keeping with the prayers of *langar* and *kar sewa*, each Sikh temple maintains a kitchen where the poor can get free meals. Members of the community volunteer to work in the kitchen, to hand out food and clean.

Indian Gods

In the main niche of Vishnu temple V at Osian, visitors can admire interpretations of heavenly beauty and gods revered by Vishnu. After rapidly growing from a dwarf into a giant, Vishnu walked through heaven, earth and the underworld in three steps in order to restore the power of the gods.

Indian gods

The stout man with the large elephant head is greeted as "Jai Ganesh." He has a tusk in one of his four hands and a scale with candy, which he adores, in another. He mostly rides composedly on a rat, or he dances – on his short, sturdy legs. He is married to Siddhi and Buddhi, insight and success. His parents are Shiva and Parvati. He is also a god, just as they are.

He is the god of wisdom and learning, the guardian of the sciences, the conqueror of all obstacles and the favorite god of all Indians. People beg for his assistance when taking exams, traveling or building a house. His statues of worship are artfully crafted on innumerable temples; red painted stones with two eyes can be seen on town squares and at road crossings and "Jai Ganesh" is personified as well with bronze figures on every home altar.

Hindus have a seemingly endless number of gods. Originally only three gods were on the same stratum at the top of the Hindu pantheon. These were Brahma as the creator, Vishnu as the guardian and Shiva as the destroyer. But Vishnu and Shiva were quickly elevated to being main gods by their respective followers while Brahma was demoted to being mediator to Vishnu at the creation of the world.

Vishnu especially is a peaceful god. Only if the world order were to become endangered would he step in to protect people from demonic powers, sometimes manifesting himself as a 'beast.' He is the scary Narasimha, half lion, half man, ripping the intestines of a recalcitrant demon from its body. The most popular forms of appearance of Vishnu are Rama and Krishna. Rama is the main character in hero and love epics and Ramayana, suppresser of the demonic force, Ravana, is the ideal image of a reliable husband and virtuous hero for Indian people. The merry Krishna is well-loved among his followers. His heroic deeds and amorous adventures can be followed on endless friezes chiseled into Indian temples, just as with the gripping tales of Rama and his wife, Sita.

Shiva looks unapproachable and enigmatic. As Nataraja, the lord of the dance, he shows himself as a god of creation. His cosmic dance symbolizes the eternal cycle of creation, destruction and recreation. Shiva is mostly revered as *lingam* (phallus) and *yoni* (vulva). These depictions refer to earlier fertility cults and symbolize the unity of Shiva and his *shakti*, which is his female energy.

The shaktas, a third important stream within Hinduism, see the origin of the universe in the female. They venerate Mahadevi, the great goddess, in numerous peaceful, heroic, virginal and wrathful forms of appearance. Durga, equipped with weapons and power from the gods, triumphed over the fertile demon king, Mahisha, when the gods could no longer overcome him themselves.

Ganesha, the beloved. Red paint, some leaves and fresh flowers transform a damaged architectural fragment into an attractive place of worship. The fact that the figure can hardly be recognized is not an obstacle. You know who you love, after all.

A ceiling portrayal of the shapes and names of Ganesha and his brother, Skanda, is in the Great Temple of Madurai. Because of his adventurous nature, it contains six heads. He is the god of war in the Hindu pantheon under his best-known names of Karttikeya (on the northern side) and Subrahmanya or Muruga (on the southern side).

1. பாலகணபதி   2. தருணகணபதி   3. பத்திகணபதி   4. வீரகணபதி   5. பிங்களகணபதி

6. உச்சிஷ்டகணபதி   7. சிப்பிரகணபதி   8. லக்ஷ்மிகணபதி   9. விக்கிநேஸ்வரகணபதி   10. ஏரம்பகணபதி

11. நிர்த்தளகணபதி   12. பூவனகணபதி   13. ஊர்த்தவகணபதி   14. சக்திகணபதி   15. துவசகணபதி

16. வல்லபகணபதி   1. சத்திதரர்   2. தண்டாயுதபாணி   3. தேவிசேநுத்பதி   4. சுப்பிரமணியர்   5. பாலகிருஷ்ணபகவான்

6. கௌவாகனர்   7. சரவணபவர்   8. கார்த்திகேயர்   9. குமாரர்   10. சண்முகர்

In the large Shiva temple of Bhojpur (Madhya Pradesh) from the eleventh century, Brahmans and pilgrams climb stairs and step onto the yoni platform, where they worship the 7.5 foot high monolithic lingam.

This three-headed Shiva on a temple in Chamba, in the Himalaya, displays a bit of his aggressive, destructive side. He is carrying a trident, a staff with a skull and an axe in three of his eight hands and dances under the elephant hide of one slain demon while trampling on another.

A good luck charm and spell-breaker for the home. On the brilliant relief in a large temple in Ellora: Shiva and Parvati can be seen in their residence on Kailash Mountain. The ten headed, multi-armed demon king, Ravana, makes the mountain tremble and is brought back to reason with one foul swoop by the big Shiva.

The god Khandoba – seen here as a mask on a small place of worship – is an example of a local god that has been 'incorporated' into the Hindu pantheon. The old shepherd god is seen as an incarnation of Shiva. The central figure of the Khandoba cult is Jejuri in Maharashtra.

In the heroic epic, *Ramayana*, Hanuman, the commander of the ape military, assists Rama to conquer the demon king, Ravana, and win back his wife, Sita. His virtues and heroic deeds make him an Indian god that is very dear to the nation.

Live portrayals from the Nayak period on the ceiling of the Parvati temple in Chidambaram (TN) portray Shiva as an ash-covered wandering beggar (Bhikshatana). He struck off one of Brahma's five heads in an eruption of rage and had to pay dearly. According to the legend, the wives of the seven Rishis brought him alms and this made him very excited.

Aiyanar has long been the guardian god of Tamil farmers. He and his companions ride through towns and fields during the night on their ghost horses to drive away evil demons. He was taken into the Hindu god's heaven later in his female form of Mohini as the son of Shiva and Vishnu. This godly infant, who lies at the feet of his parents in this modern place of worship, is venerated with fresh flowers.

Nationally protected places of worship are typically located in fields. Kshetrapala is depicted with both of his wives, his permanent companion, a dog, and a domesticated demon under his left foot.

The town is very well-protected by Durga with her lion, seven mother goddesses and the 'boss,' who is, in turn, protected by two very well-armed guards.

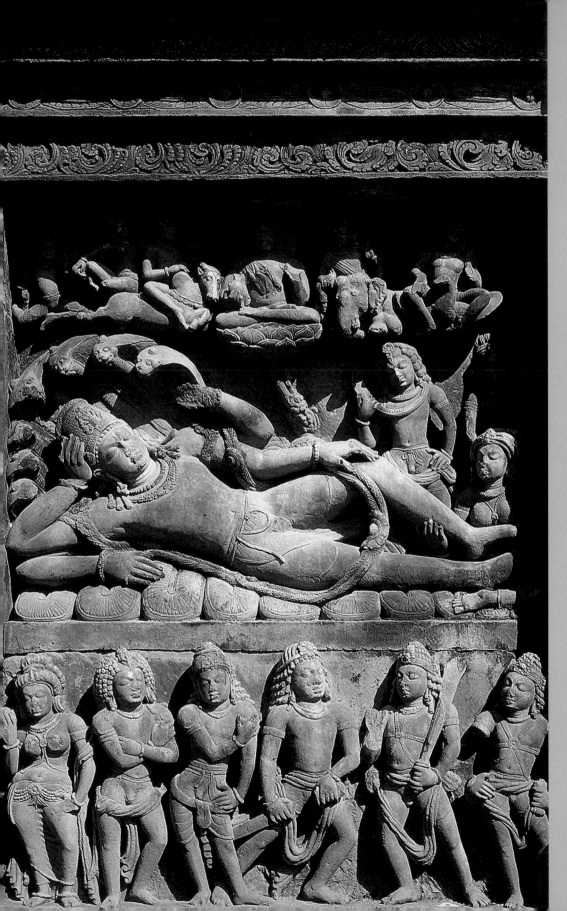

The brilliant relief on the Gupta temple of Deogarh (Uttar Pradesh) shows Vishnu resting on the snake, Shesha, and drifting between two periods of the world in the ancient ocean. Brahma is sitting on a lotus, which is actually springing from Vishnu's navel. He will recreate the world upon Vishnu's command.

Vishnu with his wife Lakshmi, the goddess of wealth, beauty and good luck. He is holding a club, a wheel, a horn shell and a lotus flower in his four hands – the four symbols that are attributed to him. Lakshmi is mostly represented with a lotus flower.

Krishna, the eighth incarnation of Vishnu on
earth, is beloved and venerated by the Indians –
as a small child, a youthful lover, the victor
over the demonic power, Kamsa, and as
the promulgator of the Bhagavadgita. In Puri,
he is presented as Jagannath, a gentleman of
the world, with his brother, Balarama, and his
sister, Subhadra. The unusual statue of worship
betrays Jagannath's ancestry from the old
Bengalese god of the fishermen. The original
sculpture is in the temple in Puri, which is only
accessible by Hindus. A copy of it is in Rajim.

The last incarnation of Vishnu is still awaited.
Kalki will appear at the end of the world,
riding on a white horse with a flaming sword
in his hand, prepared to restore order
and righteousness.

The terracotta panels on the temple in Bishnupur
(Bengaline) illustrate an event from
Krishna's youth that people like to think back
upon. He removed the clothes of a bathing
shepherdess and let her dance to cheerful flute
music under a tree.

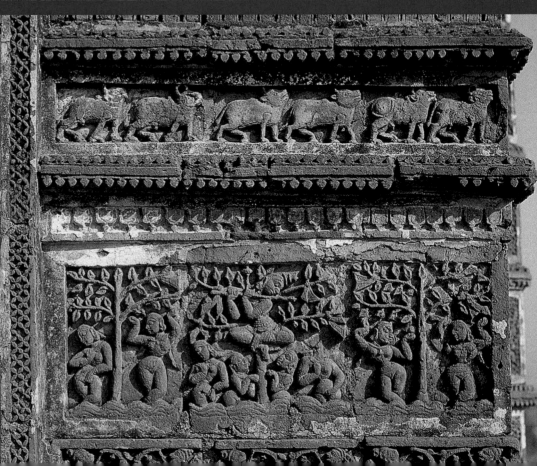

Beautiful temples were built for Surya,
the sun god, during the Middle Ages.
He is depicted as a beautiful, young man
with two lotus flowers in his hands, sitting in
a sun carriage on the Varahi temple in Chaurasi
(Orissa), which is pulled by seven horses
and steered by Aruna, the god of dawn.

Yama, a mythical king from the Indo-Aryan era
transformed into the god of death
and the adjudicator of the dead and the powers
of hell. He carries a staff with a skull and a snare
with which he pulls the soul from the body and
ties it up. He rides on a black buffalo. He is also
the protector of the world of the south at the
temple in Bhubaneshvar.

Durga is the Great Goddess and mother in whom all destructive and life-giving powers have been united. She protects the world and steps in when danger is threatening the world. The destruction of the buffalo demon, Mahisha, is one of her great deeds, depicted here on the 'Queens Stepwell' in Patan (Gujarat).

Emanating from the dreadful goddess of death, Kali found a way into Hinduism. She protects her followers and mercilessly punishes the enemies of gods and people. The 'Great Mother' is given animal sacrifices on her day of celebration.

For a few rupees you can take her home with you – the darling goddess of India.

As opposed to the precisely defined or main gods described through legend of the Hindu pantheon, Bhero, a Rajasthan omnipresent deity, is hard to define. He is represented with colorful marker stones, sometimes in precious stones or simply as a marking on the wall, in simple shrines along the way or as a 'subtenant' in temples of other gods.

Temples, cities and palaces

The palace of the Maharanas of Mewar and the surrounding *havelis* (city palaces) of the nobility and the rich merchants form the core of the city, Udaipur.
Since the seventeenth century, each monarch has added new buildings to those of their forefathers. The result is an impressive assemblage which radiates the power and splendor of the Rajput monarchs.

Temples, Cities and Palaces

The Taj Mahal is the place most people associate with Indian architecture. The Taj Mahal, built in the seventeenth century by the mogul emperor Shah Jahan, is indeed one of the most fascinating buildings on Indian soil.

At the beginning of the current era Buddhism was flourishing in India, which produced the works of art in the elevated monasteries in Karla and Ajanta. The holy district in Sanchi, with its great steps, is imposing in its portrayal of the cosmos and a powerful image from the life of Buddha at the gates. Hindu temples must also be interpreted cosmologically – a place on earth where gods and people make contact. The stuffy, dark cella in the temple, the holiest of the holy, is the deity itself. These are manifested in various decorative forms and figures on the outer walls of the temple. The North Indian Nagara style reached the epitome of its development in the thirteenth century with the temples of the Solanki in Modhera and Kiradu and the building work of the Ganga dynasty in Bhubaneshvar and Konarak. The Dravid building style was developed in South India on the basis of monolithic model temples. These masterworks were created at the beginning of the eleventh century under the Cholas in Tanjore and Gangaikondacholapuram.

The ground plans of temples and cities in ancient India were developed in the shape of a square or a rectangle. The same style is applied in the great temple cities of South India, which were built in rectangular shapes. The holiest among the relatively small, gilded towers are formed by the core, around which the city is grouped along various ring

ways. The holiness decreases as the distance to the sanctuary increases and the towers at the top of the four ports between the ring-shaped city parts become ever higher. These are decorated from top to bottom with figures of multi-armed gods, gruesome demons and main characters from mythological epic poems. A late and imposing example of a city designed in this way is the new capital city of Jaipur, built by Jai Singh in the eighteenth century.

At the end of the twelfth century, the Muslims came to power in North India. The onset of a long and fruitful development can even be seen in their first structure, the Qutb Minar in Delhi. The collusion between Hinduism and Islamic art can clearly be seen. Emperor Akbar went so far as to try and merge the two religions. Many Hindu ideas were incorporated into his structures. The Divan-i-Khas in Fatehpur-Sikri, for instance, has a beautiful central pillar – suggesting an earth axis – which supports the seat of the emperor.

The Islamic influence can also be seen in the palaces of Hindu emperors. The Man Singh palace in Gwalior, with its dome covered towers and colorfully decorated façade, is a masterwork of the synthesis between Islamic and Hindu styles. The imposing throne hall of the Nayyaks of Madurai under a wide domed ceiling would never have been built on such a scale without new techniques.

The cave monasteries of Ajanta bear witness to the primacy of Buddhism in India before the monastery complexes of Hinayana were established. The masterpieces of Mahayana Buddhism were chiseled from rocks under the Vakataka monarchs. *Chaitya* (sanctuary) no. 19, with its imposing façade, is among them.

A Buddhist stupa is not a tumulus, but a depiction of the cosmic manifestation of the world order. One of the most impressive is the Great Stupa of Sanchi. The four ports of stone enclose what is holy from the profanities of the world. Their lively reliefs are a highlight of old Indian art.

The temples of the Kiradu stand in the desolate fields of Rajasthan, close to the border with Pakistan. They mark the site of a flourishing trade center, established under the Paramaras in the eleventh century. Architecture and sculptures provide a prototype of medieval Rajput art.

A charming relief on the Someshvara temple in Kiradu: Ganesha and his shakti "arm-in-trunk." He does not let go of the plate with the candies.

Another relief on the same temple shows one of the feared 'heavy' weapons from the time: armored war elephants.

A very impressive variant of the Nagara style was developed in Khajuraho, the former capital of Chandella-Rajputs, in the tenth or eleventh century. The conic-shaped *shikhara*, which towers above the sanctuary, flanked by smaller, arched shikharas, looks like an enormous organic sprout.

The walls of the temple of Khajuraho are completely covered with rhythmically structured groups of gods, fabled creatures, couples in erotic poses and hotheaded, heavenly nymphets jumping around – such as here on the Duladeo temple.

The 194 foot high towers of the temple of Jagannath rise from the sea of houses and loom over the hall of sacrifices, the hall of dance and the audition hall in Puri. Built in the fifth century, the current temple dates back to 1198. The mighty complex has a square floor plan, encircled by hundreds of other temples.

The imposing Rajarani temple in Bhubaneshvar influenced the arts of medieval Orissa. Loving female figures were effectively removed from the finely chiseled pillars of red sandstone. In the middle is the protector of the southwestern world and the embodiment of death and destruction, Nirrita.

Dwarka, located on the western tip of the peninsula of Kathiawar, was the capital of Krishna during later years. This city is currently among the seven most important pilgrimage destinations for Hindus. The imposing Dwarkadhish temple from the thirteenth century with its five story hall and 170 foot shikhara is the center of the Krishna society in Dwarka.

Of the Surya temple on Konarak, which was designed as a sun chariot with twelve sets of wheels drawn by seven horses, only the stately main hall and the dance hall remain.

The Keshava temple in Somnathpur is the newest and most flawless of the famous Hoyshala temples in Dekhan. Three star-shaped shrines and an enclosed hall built for it stand on a plinth, the shape of which follows the exact contours of the temple.

During the seventh century, Pallave king Narasimhavarman I had native and imprisoned Chalukya craftsmen chisel miniature monolithic temples from the granite rocks found in Mamallapuram. Five of the 'Seven Pagods,' which the travelers admired earlier, have been preserved. The 'Dharmaraja-Ratha' model (second from front) was used as an example for the construction of the first temples of the Pallavas and forms the core of the Dravidic style.

The great Chola king Rajaraja I had the Brihadishvara temple in Tanjore built around 1,000 AD – a masterpiece of South Indian temple architecture. The 217 foot tower comprises the sixteen stories topped by an eighty ton heavy monolithic dome.

The eastern-most outer port towers
of the Minakshi temple in Madurai,
called Raja-Gopuram, are nine stories
(165 feet) high.

The Minakshi temple in Madurai
is a concentrically designed temple city.
A countless number of halls and towers are
arranged around the sanctuary under the
modest towers with golden domes (left).
The port towers increase in height the
further they are from the sanctuary.

In Darasuram and Konarak, the entire temple
was built according to the concept of
a procession or sun chariot and in front of the
Vithalaswami temple in Vijayanagar, is the
Garuda pavilion, made from granite into the
shape of a richly decorated temple chariot.

This bizarre building in Chanderi is known as
"Badal Mahal Gate." It is a palace port without
a palace. The fantasy building work was
completed around 1460. The reason for it is not
exactly clear.

The palace on the fortress rock of Gwalior (Madhya Pradesh), known as Man Mandir, was built around 1500 by the Rajput Empire of Man Singh. The imposing façade is divided into levels by cylindrical towers crowned with *chatris* (pavilions), or heaven-like roofs. Airy stone railings divided by the chatris and connected with elegant balconies, were decorated with blue, green and yellow glazed bricks, just as with the walls. These represent banana plants, tigers and elephants and form ornamental friezes with lancet arches and a series of depictions of ducks.

The palaces of Rajasthan 'grew' through many generations and are imposing not only from the outside. They often also contain some hidden art treasures. The Cloud palace, the residence of the Maharoas of Bundi, houses beautiful murals from the seventeenth century on the walls and ceiling in Badal Mahal. The central scene displays the god Rama with his consort, Sita, and brother Lakshmana in a type of palanquin, carried by angelic creatures, flying through heaven.

Maharadja Bir Singh Deo of Orchha built the Govinda palace in Datia (Madhya Pradesh) around 1620. The building with its mighty central towers connected to the square palace with transparent bridges is the culmination of Rajput architecture.

The Lakshmi Vilas-palace in Vadodara (former Baroda) was commissioned in 1880 by maharadja Sayajirao Gaekwad. It was completed twelve years later at a cost of eighteen million pounds. The British architect, Major Mant, was given the honorary nickname, 'Mad Mant,' due to its poignant mix of styles.

Arts and Crafts

The products of this potter are very popular all
over India. Crockery, ranging from storage
pots to cups in which train passengers are
given hot tea at stations, is widely used.

Arts and Crafts

Arts and crafts have always been a part of daily life in India as well as an essential aspect of its dynamic culture. Festivals and rites in the lives of individuals, as well as within the cycle of seasons, lead to tradesmen being commissioned to produce various articles: toys amulets, embroideries and decorative items, dishes from brass or clay, bridal chests, depictions on paper and textile, bronze holy and ritualistic objects.

These objects, dazzling with their rich colors or unique shapes, are not created impulsively. They must satisfy functional, sacred and sometimes iconographic requirements. The items give expression to uninterrupted tradition and have survived from generation to generation.

The colors, patterns and shape of the objects reveal information about the possessor, the maker, the user. In this way, the sari of a woman in Gujarat provides information about her jati, place of origin and civil status. Variations and quality of Indian textile products are evidence of the high standards of trade arts on the subcontinent. The materials range from delicate muslin, considered valuable by the Romans, to colorfully decorated chintz which enchanted Europe three hundred years ago and the brilliant brocade fabrics from Varanasi, Gujarat and Paithan. Refined ikats and batiks are originally from the deserts of West India. The women of the various tribes enhance the effect of the dyes with embroideries applied using various techniques, including sewn-on embroideries, sequins and small mirrors.

All craftsmen are said to be descendants of Vishvakarma, a god venerated during the Vedas, the architect among the gods and the forefather
of all craftsmen, painters and sculptors. Once a year, craftsmen honor
him, dedicating many tools to him. The blacksmiths, sculptors, metal
casters, stonemasons and goldsmiths are all descendants from the five
sons of Vishvakarma, according to the Holy Scriptures.

A trip through India serves to remind one of the masterworks of the
craftsmen of bygone times. Homes, temples and palaces in the Kulu
Valley, in Gujarat and Kerala are decorated with plastic sculptures. In
the temples of Chamba and Tamil Nadu, brilliantly shaped, large, bronze
statues of gods can be admired. The open-worked marble fencing and
the delicate inlay work of the palaces of the moguls and Rajput
monarchs always incur the admiration of viewers. They provide insight
into the artistic, intellectual and spiritual life of a culture; snake stones
symbolize fertility, commemorative stones symbolize fallen heroes and
sati stones are reminders of women who burnt themselves along with
the corpses of their husbands.

Crockery made on the potter's wheel and then left to dry in the sun is carefully stacked to be baked.

The Bengalese city of Bishnupur is famous for its lovely, seventeenth and eighteenth century temples which are completely covered with terracotta. This fragment of the façade of the Jore Bangla temple shows scenes from the Ramayana.

In Tamil Nadu, horses made from baked clay are offered to the gods who protect the homes and fields – especially Aiyanar. They vary from small to larger than life, shown here at Arantargi.

Artistic wood carving has a long tradition
in the forested areas of India. Delicate
embroideries, so-called *rumal*, are stretched
over lovely wooden frames in Chamba.

In the palace of the Jhala Rajput Empire
in Halwad, brilliantly cut columns support
the gallery around the large courtyard.
They are among the most beautiful Gujarat
has to offer in wood carving work.

In Veraval, on the coast of Gujarat, the same
ships which used to connect East Africa, Arabia
and India long before Vasco da Gama reached
India, are still being built: the *dhaus*.

Krishna most probably seduced the *gopis* (shepherdesses) by playing with a bamboo flute similar to the one shown here. This flute is still made today; it is used in folk music and bought by tourists.

The red cylinder in the middle of the photo is a public mailbox in Jaisalmer. The ladies and gentlemen are marionettes in the tradition of the Rajput Empire.

Despite the large variety of industrially produced replicas, beautiful bracelets are still being made in the traditional way with lacquer. This raw material is obtained by taking the sap from an indigenous tree.

Bracelets are made from camel bone in Rajasthan. Beautiful old pieces in particular are in demand by collectors. Over time, they take on different shades: from honey yellow to cognac tints, distinguishing them from imitation bracelets.

Women from India's nomadic tribes, with their colorful clothing, often adorned with small mirrors, are striking because of their love for decoration. The heavy silver hangers on both sides of the face are attached to the hair, not the ears. Old silver coins are often used for the breast piece. The women often have to perform difficult physical labor using their hands. This is probably why they prefer to wear rings around their toes.

The pride of Ladakh women is their *peraks*, the unique head covers. Today, they are mostly worn only during ceremonies. Pure turquoise stones are mounted on gold and silver decorative plates and then on a strip of leather, covered with a red substance, which runs to a point at the front and back. Richly decorated pieces can weigh up to a few pounds.

With so many temples in India richly decorated with sculptures, it is no wonder that the craft of stone sculpting continues to flourish.

Small effigies of gods and goddesses are also used at the small altars in every Hindu household. This sculptor has lost his fingers because of leprosy. His talent is clear as he is still capable of cutting beautiful ganeshas from soft soapstone.

The work of Indian sculptors is of a very high quality. Due to the presence of so many religious temples, they have to be able to work with varied materials and different styles.

Most Indian drums are played by hand.
In order to vary the tone, the drum skins are
strengthened in certain spots with a paste
of a very specific composition.

The people of Dhobini in Madhya Pradesh are
famous for making drums.

South Indian percussion instruments are used
at a temple festival in Kerala.

Details of the shikhara of the great Shiva temple from around 1060 in Udayapur (Madhya Pradesh) with very finely worked ornaments and miniature shikharas.

A stonemason uses a fragment to measure a pre-treated stone in order to copy it.

A family at work dyeing cloth on the side of the road in Lachhmangarh (Rajasthan).

Patterns are placed on delicate fabrics with hand stamps in Pindwara (Rajasthan) and left to dry in the sun.

Dancers from Jodhpur in Marwari costumes with extravagant bead adornments.

A lovely, treated *sati* stone in Karnataka.
The red paint and the prints on the stone
indicate that there is a place of worship
for Devi.

These snake stones symbolize fertility. Women
express their desire for children to the snake
stone spirits. There are images of either
a lingam, which stands for Shiva,
or of a youthful Krishna in a youthful shape
in relief between the entwined snake bodies.

Travel and Trade

Sirpur (Madhya Pradesh) is a destination for farmers. The journey is difficult with heavily laden carts: after crossing the Mahanadi River, the sandy banks loom ahead.

Travel and Trade

Street musicians in Calcutta; the singing is accompanied by a drum and a harmonium.

An Indian family, especially a Hindu family, lives in accordance with established rites of passage. After initiation rites, the first solid feeding of the child and the start of school, boys from the top three *varnas* (classes) receive holy cords during an initiation ceremony after puberty, which means that they are 'born again' and accepted into the community. They will then be able to do the same work as their fathers or follow him in business. The parents prepare their son's wedding, select a suitable bride and – after the agreement of the bride and groom – negotiate with the other parents about the bridal chest. The wedding is the most important event in a woman's life. It is held in the traditional way and as resplendently as possible. The young woman is taken into the family of her husband. Her position within the family is established with the birth of the children, especially sons. After the death of the parents, it is the duty of the children to perform long, prescribed rituals.

Times are changing, however. Today, at least in metropolitan societies, women study, young girls choose love marriages, the extravagant bridal chests are abandoned and newlyweds choose their own homes. But India is a rural country – more than three quarters of the total population live in rural areas.

The farmer's calendar is determined by the monsoons and, like city dwellers, they structure their festival days according to the season, local temple celebrations and great *melas*. Melas are temple festivals, markets, pleasant occasions and family meetings rolled into one. The gods are often honored after a day of traveling, a successful business transaction, the arrangement of a wedding or after long social contacts have been kept. A pilgrimage is a very important event in the life of a Hindu. The purpose can be Benares or Kanyakumari, but it is most often a visit with his own family to the famous temples of his personal god. The flourishing local tourism is based on pilgrimages to gods.

Many people have their fixed place in daily life, but there are also those who have to struggle on a daily basis to get something to eat. They hope to get some informal work or to trade in the bazaar. The Bazaar is the heart of the Indian community. Craftsmen who practice the same trade live and work close to each other in the same alleys. The shops of the jewelers and fabric traders are crowded along the main streets. These are long, narrow buildings, open onto the street. Wares are stacked high against the walls and the floor is covered with a beautiful 'lazy' mattress. Street vendors spread their merchandise in front of the shops and mobile restaurants provide passers-by with food. Astrologers and palm readers predict bright futures for their clients in the vicinity of the temple.

No other family celebration in India is celebrated with the same resplandence as a wedding. For the inhabitants of Rajasthan, the groom rides to the ceremony on a white horse dressed up as a maharaja. The bride awaits his arrival beautifully adorned.

The men wear turbans in the colors of their region of origin. Here, the Mewaris in Pune are celebrating. A wedding orchestra enhances the already exuberant atmosphere.

The hands of the bride and groom are covered with a shawl. After the lighting of the holy fire and the offering of butter, the priest initiates the most important part of the ceremony. The couple walks four times around the flames and makes a sacrifice to Agni, the god of fire.

Sports play a very important role in India, especially in higher education. This long-distance race is taking place in the neighborhood of Nagpur in Maharashtra.

City life in New Delhi during winter; book stalls at Connaught Place.

The Indian national sport is without a doubt cricket. Top players are adored as movie stars are. Training is taken very seriously and begins at a very young age. A scene from Chowpatty Beach in Mumbai.

The gods provided cattle because they bring people many advantages, serving as hauling animals and providing milk. Cattle dung is shaped and left to dry in the open air. It makes excellent material for fires.

Cattle dung does not smell; it is not only commonly used in households – many town smiths use it to put new iron strips around the wheels of oxcarts.

Statues of popular gods such as Ganesha, Bhero and Hanuman or Maruti, shown here, in the town of Nilgud in Maharashtra, came into existence spontaneously, and are mostly bright red. With *puja*, a worshipping ritual, they are washed with water and milk, rubbed with sandalwood paste and decorated with garlands. People bring offerings such as coconuts and flowers, spread the smoke from oil lamps and recite holy verses and prayers.

In places of pilgrimage, colored powders are used to honor the gods – mostly red or Kukuma (yellow) such as here in Jejuri. The powders are sprinkled over the statues; the faithful rub it on their foreheads or toss it into the air with cries of joy to venerate Khandoba.

The dead are honored on special days. Varkala in Kerala has a long tradition of honoring ancestors. This ceremony takes place on the beach. Small offerings are sanctified, taken to the water and thrown ceremoniously into the sea.

Temple festivities have a unique quality in South India. Here in Panavally, Kerala, seventy-five beautifully decorated elephants are brought together to venerate the goddess Ambika.

Pushkar Mela: puja in the Brahma temple, a bath in holy water, doing business, meeting family, speaking to friends and all sorts of activities. The *sadhus*, as well as their lucky cow with a fifth hoof on its back, participate.

Pilgrimage to the temple of Srinathji in Nathdwara – and a tattoo of Krishna as a memento?

Markets are also places where information is exchanged among inland tribes at Orissa. The ikatsaris of the women with their green and white tints can be seen clearly here.

Ancestor veneration in Rajasthan:
A procession of women carry pots filled with
holy water from the Ganges on their heads.
Some younger women fall into trances when
the forefathers take possession of them,
thus making contact with their children,
grandchildren and great-grandchildren.

Religious and world affairs are openly discussed. In Sri Rangam (Tamil Nadu), the outer wall of the temple complex, directly next to the main entrance, serves as a massive information board for the local cinema.

Traffic islands are not used for regulating traffic at this crossing in the old center of Udaipur, but as pit stops for the city's people and cattle who want to relax and contemplate.

Dabawallahs in action. Four thousand people from 'Mumbai Tiffin Box Suppliers' ensure day in and day out that 125,000 hungry employees and workers get lunch at their place of work. Transferring areas are the biggest stations, such as here at Churchgate Station.

Whether it is steaming hot or rainy, the bazaar always entices shoppers.

At the bazaar, a woman climbs on a table at a jeweler's to try on a toe ring.

Traveling through India

Maharashtra and Goa

The cave monasteries of Ajanta are among the most important examples of Buddhist art in India. Twenty-nine caves are lined up in a wide half circle on the steep shore of the Waghora River. The five oldest date back to the first and second centuries BC. The third was made around the fifth and sixth centuries. The seventeenth cave from this period is, as the main scene of the veranda of the *vihara* (temple) shows, decorated with expressive art.

153

Maharashtra and Goa

The 'Gateway of India' is the colonial triumphal arch at the harbor of Mumbai, where prominent visitors entered India when it was under British rule – and it is also where the last British soldier left India in 1948. The 'Gateway of India' includes the entire city. The city of Bombay came about in the seventeenth century on seven malaria infected islands, the first piece of 'British India.' The first Asian train went on the Bombay-Thane line in 1853. Bombay was connected to Calcutta ten years later. Mumbai is currently a confident metropolis with a whopping sixteen million inhabitants who represent 38 percent of India's gross national product. Mumbai is proud to be the most active film producing city in the world, but less proud of having the largest slums in Asia.

Only a few miles from Mumbai, the rising West Ghats constitute an imposing backdrop. This mountain range rises abruptly to heights of roughly 4,900 feet. Both of the important mountain passes start in Mumbai, conquer the barrier at a height of 2,300 feet and lead to the Dekan plateau with its distinctive plateau mountains and broad valleys which stretch inland for an immeasurable distance. Cotton, tobacco, wheat, rice and sugarcane flourish in its fertile soil; millet and peanuts thrive in its less fertile soil.

The mountain crest and the ravines of the Ghats are covered in red laterite and are densely wooded in parts. The inhospitable Shivaji land is where the Marathen resisted the Mongols in the seventeenth century. Impregnable mountain fortresses were built here. They gradually conquered the land and established a mighty state. For centuries,

under the Peshwars, Hindu temples were built. A new style symbolizing the renaissance of an independent national culture came into existence.

The famous cave monasteries and rock temples mark the beginning, as well as the culmination, of the history of art in Maharashtra. At the beginning of the era, early rock monasteries were established under the patronage of the Satavahanas of Paithan in Ajanta, Kondane, Karle, Baja and Bedsa, among others. During the third and sixth centuries, the Hindus in Vakatakas also supported Mayana Buddhism. Caves of worship with beautiful murals and sculptures have been preserved in Ajanta and Ellora. Those in Ellora are in a true open air museum of early Indian rock building and sculpture. The loveliest of all the Hindu temples were made during the eighth century here and in Elephanta in Mumbai.

The old cultural landscape of Konkan stretches out between the Ghats and the sea – with its own language and open culture. The constituent state of Goa, which borders Maharashtra to the south, was under Portuguese influence for a long time due to their long reign in the area. The imposing relics from those glorious days make an impression upon visitors, but the open, Mediterranean lifestyle of the Goanese also makes this small piece of land very pleasant.

The center of old Bombay is formed by the 'Fort' city with its harbor. The lovely buildings of the British Empire stand here – an eclectic mixture of European and oriental styles over the centuries. The panorama shows the Taj Mahal Hotel from 1903 on the left with its modern extensions. The Gateway of India next to it marks the place where illustrious visitors to India – such as King George V and Queen Mary – landed. The brilliant domes belong to the Prince of Wales Museum and the GPO (General Post Office), among others.

The beautiful building of the Municipal Corporation, the city hall, was built in 1893.

Mumbai's red light district is located in the heart of the old inner city around Falkland Road. Many of the prostitutes come from the tribal (adivasi) areas of India or from neighboring countries such as Nepal and Burma.

The cages of the prostitutes, located along the streets, and the barred doors create a sense that there are cages everywhere.

Between the city parts of Fort, with its colonial atmosphere, and the old inner city, the British established Mumbai's famous Crawford Market, now known as Mahatma Jyotiba Phule Market, in 1871. Homemakers and traders buy fruit, flowers, vegetables, herbs and spices, meat, poultry and fish here. Live animals such as cats and parrots can be traded here as well. The young boys with the baskets make a living by carrying people's shopping.

Hijras. Hermaphrodites or eunuchs in women's clothes venerate the goddess, Yellamma, through prostitution. They dance in her honor and carry altars dedicated to her on their heads.

The decorative building style of the Persian temples in the business district indicated the Persian influence all over Mumbai. On the footpath in front of the temple, furniture makers and carpenters offer their services.

Malabar Hill was popular as a suburb during colonial rule, where these labor intensive 'launderettes' were established.

The famous Shiva sanctuary of Elephanta
from the sixth or seventh century is located
on an island just over six miles from Mumbai.
The impressive panels with scenes from
the Shiva legend and the gigantic watchmen
on the hollest part (photo) of this great temple
are very imposing, despite the damage done
to it by embrasures dug by the Portuguese
in the sixteenth century.

Hidden in the narrow valley of the Ghats,
between Mumbai and Pune, is the Buddhist
monastery of Kondane. The well-preserved
façade of the *chaitya* hall as well as the
worship and prayer area from the second
century BC indicate that wooden huts were
used as models.

One of the masterworks in relief in the Dash Avatara cave depicts Vishnu in the form of a boar. A demon stole the Vedas of the sleeping Brahma and pulled the surface of the earth to the bottom of the ocean. We see how Vishnu – in the form of the earth goddess, Bhu – rescues the earth and tramples the rebellious Yaksha.

The Kailasha temple at Ellora, meant to be a depiction of the mountain of gods in the Himalayas, is among the places of worship dedicated to Shiva.
India's large rock sanctuary was hacked from hard volcanic rock in the shape of a South Indian temple over a surface of 197 x 295 x 98 feet. The people simply left the building and all of its decorations in place – only the stones around it were removed.

Beautiful reliefs, such as this one depicting heavenly creatures floating along in 'knee flight,' decorate the impressive façade.

Cave ten is the only Buddhist sanctuary with a Chaitya hall. It has three beech trees, an apse with a large stupa and a Buddha statue in the front.

The Vakaris form the most popular alignment of the Vishnu society in Maharashtra. Twice a year they make a pilgrame to Pandharpur to worship Vithoba and his wife, Rukmini, in their temple. Their spiritual leaders have lived here since the thirteenth century, from the time of the famous holy poet of Jnaneshvar, whose portrait the pilgrims carry with them, to Ramdas, the guru of Shiva's worshippers.

Nasik is located by the holy river, Godavari.
It is one of the four cities on which a few drops
of the immortality potion spilled during
the battle waged between the gods
and the demons for possession of the potion.
Thus hundreds of thousands of visitors journey
here for Kumbh Mela every twelve years –
interchanged with Ujjan, Hardwar
and Allahabad. Pilgrims also visit the areas
outside these festival periods. Many can be
seen by the river.

Stalls with mountains of shining pigments
can always be found at popular pilgrimage
resorts. *Kumkum*, the red powder, is often used:
women paint the crown of their heads and
men their foreheads. As the puja (the service
at the temple) takes on an ecstatic character,
the religious start moving homeward, covered
from top to bottom with red dust.

In the area of the Mahabaleshvar, an ancient place of worship demarcates the source of five Dekan rivers, among them the Krishna. The water source springs from a stone, forming lovely steps in the basin.

Mahabaleshvar, Maharashtra's highest hill station at 4,500 feet, is located in the very romantic Sahyatri Mountains of West Ghats. Indian visitors love the dramatic viewpoints (Sunrise, Sunset and others) explored by the British in 1828. Arthur's Seat is one of the most spectacular.

Mirya Bay is a picturesque fishing area in the regional capital of Ratnagiri by the Arabic Sea. Fish caught in abundance are sold directly on the beach. The highest prices are paid for butterfish, the favorite dish in Mumbai restaurants.

Mahuli is located where the Krishna and Yenna flow together. During the height of the Maratha Empire in the eighteenth century, extensive and complicated temples were built. They have their own style which combines elements from North and South Indian arts. Dipa-mala, a sail which is hung out during festivals with oil lamps, is essential.

As large hotels and beach resorts pop up along the beaches of Goa, many nature lovers and romantic souls move further away – preferably to the south. The dreamy Palolem beach is still untouched, but souvenir traders have already swooped down upon it.

A few of the beautiful churches of Goa, which do not need to take a backseat to Rome and Lisbon, are still left. Only half of the 151 foot Augustine monastery has been left standing.

Karnataka

Sadhus are associated with India. Real
sadhus are traveling ascetics. They belong to
different – mostly Shivatic – sects. The silver
linga holder carried on his chest indicates
that he is a member of the lingayats.

Karnataka

The fine beach sand that makes the Goa so attractive stretches for hundreds of miles along neighboring Karnataka. These are used exclusively by fishermen, with the exception of Gokarn in the north and Maravanthe and Ullal in the south. The varying heights of the West Ghats mountain range follow the coast. The monsoon season has a profound impact on the area, providing a maximum of 13 feet of rain per year. Coconut palms provide the environment with a distinctive character. Cashew and areca nuts are cultivated here. On the other side of the mountain crest are extensive forests which cover 20 percent of the territory of this constituent state. Large areas with fertile soil are found in the north at the Dekan plateau, which becomes even more impressive further north as it is interchanged with impressive rock landscapes on thin granite. Grain, cotton, legumes, sugar cane and tobacco are all cultivated there. Near the extended areas in Vijayanagar, spotted with ruins, opulent banana plantations are found wherever there is water.

The constituent state of Karnataka was founded in 1956 from the principality of Mysore and is expanded with a few Kannada-speaking areas of neighboring regions. Bangalore became the capital city instead of the old residential city of Mysore. This city was established by royals and developed at a fast rate into a center of modern technology, aircraft manufacturing and space exploration technology. Bangalore is currently known as the Silicon Valley of India because of its software industry.

During the sixth and seventh centuries AD, the so-called Early Westerly Chalakyas developed into a major force in Dekan. The capital of Vatapi/Badami and Pattadakal and Aihole bear witness to the high culture of this artistic Hindu dynasty. Rashtrakuta's Dekan ruled in the centuries after, followed by the Late Westerly Chalukyas in the tenth century. As the power of these rulers declined at the end of the twelfth century, many left the region.

The Yadavas in the north and the Kakatiyas in the south withdrew and the empire of the Hoysalas was established in the southern Karnataka around their capital of Dorasamudra/Halebid. They followed in the architectural traditions of the Chalukyas in the second century, but reshaped it into their own style. The collapse of the political order in Dekan at the end of the thirteenth century worked in the favor of the attacking Muslims and they forced them to the south. With the establishment of the Hindu Vijayanagar Empire, development was delayed once again. The Bahmani Empire was established around the same time and the Dekan sultans who followed developed into deadly opponents of the Vijayanagar. The battle of 1565 at Talikota uit was a disaster. The forces of Vijayanagar were defeated and one hundred thousand people lost their lives. The capital was plundered and destroyed.

What survived is included on the world heritage lists and is deemed among the most fascinating sights of Karnataka, alongside the capitals of the Dekan sultans: Gulbarga, Bidar and Bijapur.

Gokarn, a town on the coast with its holy prana lingam, a Hindu sanctuary, and lovely, wide beaches is recommended for backpackers. The women of Halaki Gowda are very striking with their unique clothing and lovely adornments.

The coast of Karnataka is bordered by hundreds of miles of white beaches with coconut plantations. Bhatkal, which has always been an important harbor for importing, is now a dreamy fishing village with a few charming and uniquely shaped temples from the Vijayanagar era.

The tile decorations on the façade are remnants of the grand *madrasa* (Islam school) of Gavan, the Persian ruler of the Sultans, who built it around 1472 in the style of the Timurid era.

Bidar succeeded as the capital of the Bahmani and Baridi sultans. This city was protected by mighty walls and and dominated by an imposing fortress.

Badami has been known as Vatapi, capital of the mighty Chalukya Empire. The city is located at the foot of steep rocks which surround a drainage basin shaped like a horseshoe. Caves used for worshipping and temples with brilliantly decorated sculptures bear witness to past glory.

The builders of the early Chalukya kings built somewhat experimental temples before they started building in their own style. They built the Bubanatha temple by the lake in the South Indian style.

The Pampapati temple is the only sanctuary that survived the plunder of the city of Vijayanagar in 1565. The 170 foot gopuram rises up somewhat bizarrely in a landscape strewn with granite blocks and ruins. According to legend, Shiva Virupaksha married the highly ranked local goddess, Pampa, the personification of the Tungabhadra River, here. He became Pampapati, the spouse of Pampa. Each year, a number of weddings are held during the winter wedding season in honor of the gods.

The town of Hampi nestled in between the ruins
of the former metropolis of Vijayanagar.
The inhabitants make use of the granite blocks
surrounding them. The ancient pavilion
by the river has become the local laundromat.

The *tabla* players and the youthful dancer have
undertaken something major: Shiva is an
ascetic god. Felt on the hair, a leopard skin and
a snake around the neck, as the lord of the
dance, Nataraj, he destroys the old world while
dancing, creating a new one at the same time.

A Brahman is taking collections for Vishnu at the entrance of the sanctuary, flanked by two beautifully crafted entrance guards.

The temples of the Hoyshala Dynasty in the southern Karnataka are masterpieces of Indian art. The area also attracts Indian tourists and is greatly admired.

Sravana Belgola is one of the holiest pilgrimage sites of the jainas and the center of the digambaras, 'who are dressed by the air' in South India. Bahubali has been standing naked, just like the monks of this sect, on the Indragiri rock since 980. He was the son of the first tirthankara of the jainas and the brother of the ancient father of India, Bharata. He is represented by a 57.4 foot statue hacked from just one block of granite. Because of his great height, worshippers communicate with his toes.
The monkey is protected in India, whether it is a black masked entellus, a type of langur, or a rhesus monkey. They have a mighty protector in the order of the gods in the ape general Hanuman, after whom the hulman has been named. Rama helped the monkey king, Sugriva, return to the throne by sending a monkey army under Hanuman to Lanka. Sita wanted to rescue from the hands of Ravana, the demon king.

Hidden in the valley of the Ghats, between Mumbai and Pune, is the Buddhist monastery of Kondane. Wooden huts were clearly used as models, as we can see from the well-preserved façade of the *chaitya* hall, the worshipping and prayer area from the second century BC.

Kerala and Tamil Nadu

The theme in Madurai is Vishnu concluding the wedding between Minakshi and Shiva – depicted on a *gopuram* of the great temple.

Kerala and Tamil Nadu

The deep south of India is the land of the dark-skinned Dravids. They most probably lived on the border of the Indus before the Aryas, who came from the north, drove them further south. They boast a long cultural history and know how to maintain maximum autonomy from the central government located so far away.

High mountain ridges which are continuations of the West Ghats form the border between the tropical Kerala and the substantially drier Tamil Nadu. To the north of the plains is Pallakkad, the most important connection between the west and the east, and the mighty mountain mass of the Nilgiri Hills. To the south is the Anaimudi in the Cardamom mountain range, reaching a height of 8,842 feet. The ends of the mountains form Cape Comorin, the southernmost point of India.

Both of these states came about through the former British Madras Presidency and they obtained their definitive borders in 1956 on the basis of language divisions. The Malayalam-speaking Kerala region stretches for 345 miles along the Malabar Coast, where the southwestern monsoons of the subcontinent stop due to the mountain barrier.

The alternating greens of coconut palms and rice fields are a feature of this coastal region. Cacao, coffee, rubber, tea, pepper, cardamom and other vegetation is grown on the slopes of the mountains. According to legend, the apostle Thomas established his first congregation on this coast. Nestorian and Syrian Christians, Jews and Arabic Muslims established themselves here in the sixth century. What a melting pot!

All lived harmoniously with the Hindus for centuries. Vasco da Gama landed at Cochino in 1498, marking the start of the colonial period. The Dutch drove the Portuguese off and later were replaced by the British. Kerala is the most populated part of India, but the population growth has been reduced to nearly zero. Around 95 percent of the inhabitants can read and write; the highest percentage in India. The communists and congress party are the leading parties in their parliament.

Tamil Nadu gets most of its rain by way of a detour from the great rivers and infrequently from the north eastern monsoon. Great dynasties took turns ruling large parts of the land for centuries on end. The Palayas in the south next to the Pandyas ruled the land from the fifth to the ninth centuries. They traded with the Greeks and Romans and brought Buddhism to South East Asia. Their cultural achievements can be admired in Kanchipuram and Mahaballipuram. The Cholas of Tanjavur ruled the land for 250 years. They conquered Burma, Malaysia, Java and Sumatra – with the sword – and likewise left very rich cultural heritage. Under the sovereignty of Vijayanagar, everything was greatly exceeded in number, height and length.

The population density of Tamil Nadu is not as high as that of Kerala, but the population is on the rise. Around 64 percent of the people here can read and write. Politics are dominated by pro-Dravid parties – preferably led by deserving godly and heroic interpreters from the Tamil films.

When the Europeans landed here in Kochi for the first time, gigantic wooden structures for sink nets, taken from the water every few minutes, already existed. Chinese fishermen, who cooperated with local traders during the era of Kublai Khan, brought their special fishing techniques with them.

Beautiful houses from the Victorian era stand along the main channel in Alappuzha. The people here build in the traditional style — with a hint of the modern.

Some prior knowledge of pantomime and the use of color cannot hurt if you want to follow the progress of a *kathakali* performance. (Those with green faces are always the 'good guys!)' All of the roles are played by men. Before the performance you can see the long process of transformation into a witch, a seductive beauty or a king.

The backwaters form their own universe. Channels become straight avenues offering stunning vistas of the rice paddies planted in the water. Lakes look like squares with traffic crossing in every direction. The torsos of two gigantic procession horses stand next to an avenue of water.

The land where pepper is grown lies to the east of the backwaters. Cacao, rubber, coffee, tea and cardamom, of course, where the mountains got their name from, are also grown there. In Kumily, cardamom is sorted during the harvest and in Kochi you can smell pepper before you see the women working with it.

Kanyakumari is at the southern point of India. Two rock islands are just behind the fishers' harbor by the coast. A temple of the great holy, philosopher and reformer Vivekananda is on one of these islands. The other island also acquired a site in the last few years: a colossal statue of the Tamil poet, Thiruvalluvar – with a panoramatic terrace.

The Communist Party CPI(M) has been a part of the government of Kerala for years. Advertising Slogons, such as here at a party congress in Thiruvannantha-puram may seem outdated and romantic to western visitors.

People come to the Great Temple of Madurai to meet the gods and bring them fresh flowers. But they also come here to reflect, to parade over the courtyard and galleries, to be looked at and to talk to each other.

Tirumalai Nayak gained its independence from the Vijayanagar Empire in the middle of the seventeenth century. They demonstrated their new powers by building a palace of truly enormous dimensions. Standing under the mighty sails of the throne hall would make anyone philosophical.

Exposed, eroded granite bits and groups of
palmyras that stand close to each other
are features if not large parts of Tamil Nadu.

Outside the towns, often under old trees, are
places of worship, mainly for local gods such as
Aiyanar or the 'seven sisters.'

The Ragunatha temple, a center of Vishunism, stands on an island in the Cauvery River in Sri Rangam. Well-known holy men and philosophers have lived here, such as Ramanuja in the twelfth century. Temple Brahmans live around the sanctuary. Just like many other Vishnu worshippers, they wear the sign of their god on their foreheads.

Long passage ways in the nearby Shiva temple lead to the holiest part where Nandi, Shiva's riding animal, rests.

Gangaikondacholapuram – 'city of the Chola that owns the water of Ganges' – is what the powerful Chola king, Rajendra I, named his new capital. Only the beautiful temple with its 197 foot tower, has withstood the centuries. The statues are among the most beautiful that Indian sculptors have ever made.

(l.) Shiva as Natharaj, the lord of the dance.

(r.) Shiva as Ardhanarishvara, the male and female aspects of godliness in one person.

One of the largest temple complexes in India is in Tiruvannamalai, where Shiva appeared in the shape of a fire soul for Brahma and Vishnu. Impressive port towers loom over the statue. The principle temple is in the middle.

Madras, the current Chennai, is an early British settlement and was enlarged into an important commercial center. The fanciful, colonial-style buildings, such as the station and the palace of justice, are characteristic of the capital of Tamil Nadu.

Andhra Pradesh and Orissa

Women from the mountain tribes of southern Orissa on their way to the market at Kudumulugumma.

Andhra Pradesh and Orissa

'Land of the Andhras' is the constituent state that borders Karnataka to the east, named after the legendary nation which emperor Ashoka had heard so much about. The sloping plains of the Dekan plateau with its scarcely populated, granite landscapes flow from low hilltops from the Eastern Ghats and the coastal plains to the Gulf of Bengal. The old cultural landscape of Telengana and the fertile swamp deltas of Krishna and Godavari border the area to the north. Andhra Pradesh was established in 1956 from the Telugu-speaking northern regions of the Madras Presidency and the powerful region of the *nizam* (sovereign) of Hyderabad.

At the beginning of the era, impressive Buddhist settlements such as Amaravati and Nagarjunakonda along the shores of the Krishna, were founded under the dynasty of the Satavahanas. Early Hindu temples of the Chalukyas in the Godavari delta and in Alampur were surrendered in the seventh century. The Kakatiyas ruled in Telengana for two hundred years, starting in 1110. Palampet and the capital of Warangal bear witness to the brilliance of this period. After that, the Bahmani sultans and then the Qutb Shahi sultans from Golkonda ruled the land. In 1590, sultan Muhammad Quli Qutb Shah established the new capital, Hyderabad, which was later extended into a splendid metropolis by the nizams.

Initially, in 1947, the dynasty wanted to remain independent, but they later decided that they wanted to become part of Pakistan. The young Indian army prevented them, however. The Congress Party is the ruling entity at the moment – after an intermezzo of the film hero, Rama Rao, with his Telugu Desam party. The Muslims, who live in the constituent state at a minority of ten percent, mostly live in the capital. They speak Urdu. This city, with its six million inhabitants and flourishing computer and software industry, is serious competition for Bangalore.

Orissa is a small constituent state with only 32 million inhabitants. The people speak Oriya, a North Indian language. The area consists mostly of uninhabitable mountainous areas that are covered with bush. 25 percent of the population lives here, referred to as the Adivasis, originating from many different tribes. These areas used to form rough, protective walls between the civilized center and the fertile plains around the mouth of the Mahanadi and Brahmani. During the fourth century, the Kalinga kings ruled the land and sea from here. Ashoka put an end to this empire one hundred years later. The bloody battle caused the Maurya emperor to convert to Buddhism and transformed him into a peace-loving sovereign. Very capable rulers led the Orissa to prosperity and power from the eighth century. This glorious period reached a crescendo during the twelfth century when they ruled over the eastern Gangas. The center of Bhubaneshvar was adorned with seven thousand temples around the Bindu Sagar tank. A temple was built in Puri for the mighty Jaganath and another temple was built in Konarak for Surya. The sultan of Bengal attacked the land in the sixteenth century and later on, so did the Mogus. After a short period with the Maraths, the British took the reigns in 1803 and ruled the land through numerous rajas.

A view from the cave temples of Undavalli over the fertile landscape of the Krishna below.

The places of worship of Bhairavakonda are located in the hills of the Velikonda Mountains in Andhra Pradesh. Brilliant statues of gods and guards, as well as pillars with sitting lions as shafts are reminders of the Pallava dynasty.

Tirupati pilgrims taking a break on their way home.
It will take a while for the hair they offered to Vishnu to grow back.

Many bonds are made in Guntur, district capital and traffic junction – to the joy of the young 'worker' who is taking a break.

The sun sets behind the dome tombs and mosques of the Qutb Shahi sultans of Golkonda.

The way ends at the wide river bed of the Krishna in Amaravati.

In 1590, Quli Qutb Shah from Golkonda established a new capital with Char Minar as the center. The 174 foot complex became the symbol of Hyderabad.

The north-south axis of the old Hyderabad houses the most prominent bazaar of the city.

The once nomadic Lambadis are becoming increasingly settled. Women offer their services in the cities as construction workers, carriers and other difficult jobs.

'Dhobis' collect dirty laundry in India. The women of this caste are drying the laundry on granite rocks ground smooth by wind and water.

Members of tribes from outlying areas meet
each other at the Kudumulagumma market.
The men hand their weapons to police
at the entrance of the market – spear, bow
and arrow – and peacefully go about bargaining
prices for chilies and garlic. The Bondas women
are very striking. They wear only loincloths, but
make up for it with rich adornments.

Fishermen's wives see their husbands off every morning to brave the waves and respectfully greet the rising sun on the nearby beaches.

The famous temple for the sun god in Konarak was built in the image of the chariot drawn by seven horses on which Surya rides through heaven every day. Twelve sets of wheels 'carry' the dado of the temple. Very fine reliefs with happy musicians, dancers and erotic groups cover the entire complex.

The Mukteshvara temple from the tenth century is a jewel among the roughly five hundred temples at Bhubaneshvar. The fascinating port archway at the entrance is a unique masterpiece.

The 'Grand Road' in Puri is the procession street along which Jaganath rides in beautifully decorated chariots with his brother and sister from the temple to his summer residence at the other end of the street. It is also a very important bazaar and communication center for the city.

A sadhu has settled at the caves of Udaigiri and taken pity on a damaged building sculpture. He clothed and decorated her – and she helps him to finance his ascetic existence.

Adivasis in the inland of Orissa lead a meager existence as self-sufficient people as tenants or farmhands for the *zamindars*, the rich land owners, on small pieces of not very fertile land.

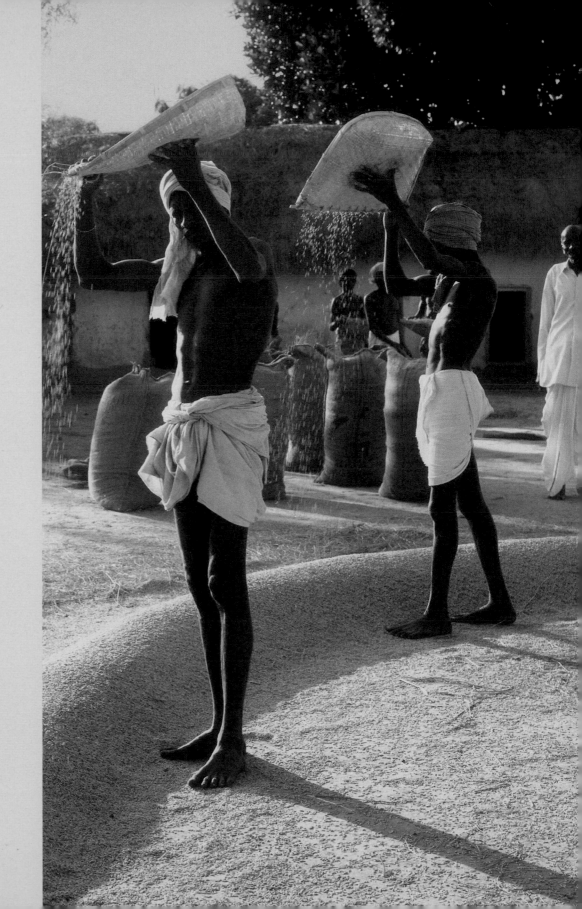

West Bengal, Bihar and Uttar Pradesh

Activities on the shore of the holy Ganges at Varanasi start at sunrise. The Brahmans on their podium chat while they await their first clients.

249

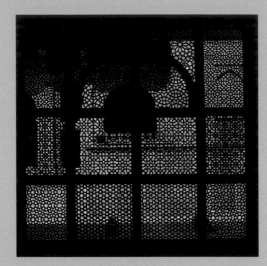

West-Bengalen, Bihar and Uttar Pradesh

The plains stretching along the Ganges and its tributaries are the economical and cultural heart of India. A unique civilization has been developing here ever since the first millennium BC. In the sixth century BC, the great Magadha Empire blossomed here. Kashi/Benares was already an important religious center for Brahmanism. In 331 BC, the Mauryas took power and captured the capital of Pataliputra/Patna. Buddha and Mahavira moved into the area, battling to enlighten people and spread their doctrine, leading to the widespread embrace of Buddhism and Jainism. Trade along the 'Great Trunk Road' flourished under Emporer Ashoka from Taxila in the west to the Gulf of Bengal in the east – and from there to Rome and Greece. The fourth and fifth centuries, the peak of the Gupta Empire, are seen as the Golden Centuries of India.

This old civilization gradually declined with the raids of Mahmud of Gazni in the eleventh century, the march of the Afghans to Bengal, the establishment of Islamic states and finally with the establishment of the Mogul Empire in 1526. A new culture came about, in no way less beautiful. Agra, the mighty fortress, was built by Emperor Akhbar, alongside a new residence, Fatihpur Sikri, and he designed his own imposing tombstone in Sikandra. His grandchild, Shah Jahan, outdid all of these masterworks with the Taj Mahal – one of the most beautiful constructions in the world.

The foundation of such development lies in the rich economic resources of the landscape. The grandiose irrigation systems devel-

oped centuries ago in the plains of Ganges and Jamuna, currently known as Uttar Pradesh, are still in use, especially for crops of wheat, barley and oats. Towards the east, in Bihar and especially in Bengal, rice plantations are still planted due to the excessive rainfall there. Tea plantations around Darjeeling and the production of jute are of great importance to Bengal, just as with any other constituent state of the Himalaya that stretches to the sea.

Uttar Pradesh has the most inhabitants in the Republic of India. Agriculture is its most prominent source of income. Only 10 percent of the population works in industry. The government is dominated by the Hindu Party nationalist, BJP, allegedly the cause of tension between Hindus and Muslims and for the uncertainty which puts a shadow on their everyday relations. Despite its natural riches, Bihar is one of the poorest and most lagging constituent states in India. Only 40 percent of its people are literate. The government was dominated for a long time by a cartel of landowners. Under the new government headed by Laloo Prasad Yadav, elected in 1991 despite his low caste origins, things were meant to get better. However, the conflict escalated. Maoist guerrilla fighters, private armies of the largest land owners, police and various castes battled relentlessly. The communists of the Marxist league in West Bengal have worked for peace, but have not achieved economic prosperity. The communists of the Marxist-Lenin league, the Naxalites, preach revolution, to no avail. The CPI is currently vying for power with the 'novices' of the Trinamul Congress.

The Victoria Memorial is the most prominent
construction in Calcutta (Kolkatta).
It was opened in 1921 – a tribute to the glory
of the British Empire.

Rickshaws, which are pulled by people at
a walking pace, can still be found in parts of
Calcutta. This is slave labor that is profitable
only during the monsoon period when
motorized traffic is rendered impossible
by the floods.

Outside popular temples, groups of beggars
congregate, hoping for generous handouts.

Bengal is the center of the Kali society in India.
A statue of this dreadful mother goddess stands
at the holiest temple of Kalighat in Calcutta.
Animal sacrifices are brought to her on a daily
basis – especially on Kalipuja and Durga-Puja
festival days.

Seventeenth and eighteenth century terracotta art flourishes in the Bengali city of Bishnupur, the ancient capital of the Malla kings. The walls of the temples are completely covered with tiles that depict, in relief, refreshingly live scenes with great epos. The fragment on the façade of the Keshta-Raya temple depicts the heroic deeds of the young Krishna, including how he killed the horse demon and suppressed the buffalo demon.

The Mahabodhi temple in Bodhgaya is a reminder of Buddha and the enlightenment he received while sitting under a bodhi tree, a late descendant of which stands directly behind the temple. Monasteries from all Buddhist countries and the most important schools of Tibetan Buddhism stand in the vicinity of the temple. There is also a large colony of Tibetans living in exile who perform their rituals in the temple area.

Water chestnuts, which look like black devil heads, are harvested in November and December and sold everywhere.

An astonishing amount of fish and other delicious water creatures are found in lakes and puddles left by the monsoon.

Everyone is equal in the eyes of the sadhus – pilgrims, traders, buyers and spectators – as long as they are willing to spend a few rupees on their spectacular show.

The place where Vishnu prevented Moksha Gajendra, a gigantic crocodile, from pulling the lord of the elephants into the water and killing him is the site of the largest cattle market in India. Everything is traded in Sonpur – from singing birds to elephants.

Varanasi is the holiest of the seven holy cities in India. Pilgrims come from all over the country to wash themselves in the Ganges. They take a ritual bath at one of the prescribed ghats: diving into the holy river, washing their mouths with the water and reciting a specific prayer. They then walk along an appointed route around the city of Shiva.

People do not only bathe and pray at the *ghats* along the river. Washers also work here. Wrestlers train their oiled bodies here. Healers demonstrate both ayurvedic healing methods and massages. Beggars recite their heartrending tales to those who pause to listen. People who die in the Varanasi are burnt at the ghats, which increases their chances of being reincarnated.

The Taj Mahal is considered the most beautiful building in India. The clear lines and noble proportions of the tombstone for the cherished wife of Mogul emperor Shah Jahan are embellished with supremely perfect decorative elements: red sandstone, geometric ornaments, shallow marble reliefs of flowers (white on white), inlay work with semi-precious stones or artfully shaped stone gril-lage in the windows.

The three storey mausoleum of the great Mogul emperor, Akbar, does not have a dome. The cenotaph stands in the open air. You can look at the port complex while walking on the galleries. Emperor Akbar had his new capital, Fatehpur Sikri, built on the place where a holy male predicted the birth of his three sons. The architect of the complex clearly sought to mix Islam and Hindu architectural styles.

Madhya Pradesh

The holy river, Narmada, springs at Amarkandak in the Maikala Mountains. The eleven points of a group of snow white temples are dreamily reflected in the water of the source pond.

Madhya Pradesh

Madhya Pradesh is not only the 'land in the middle' as its name indicates; it is also the largest constituent state in India. Its size was reduced in 2000, however. The southeastern part of Chhattisgarh became an independent constituent state under that name. The geographical profile of both constituent states is greatly varied. High lying plateaus and steep mountain ridges are divided by deep river valleys. The slopes are often thickly wooded. This landscape barrier has divided the northern cultures from South India and it has impeded conquest expeditions for centuries.

The lives of the people are mostly influenced by agriculture. Fertile black soil lies on the Malwa plateau to the west. Cotton, wheat, sugarcane, millet and peanuts are cultivated here. The bush, which covers around 30 percent of the ground surface, is an important economic factor. Coal and various metals are mined in the east. The richest coal and ore deposits are found in Chhattisgarh, however, leading to the establishment of an industrial center over the past fifty years. Enormous steel factories were built under Nehru with development funds from Durg and Bhilai. The vast stream landscape of the Mahanadi and its tributaries, where the largest industrial cities are located, is also a very fertile area for growing rice.

The earliest remnants of human settlement in Madhya Pradesh are found south of the capital, in Bhopal: the living and colorful rock paintings from the Stone Age of Bhimbetka.

The land has always formed part of great empires and local dynasties vying for power. Ujjain in Malwa has been one of the seven holy cities for Hindus since 500 BC. The early Buddhist masterworks of Sanchi came about under the Mauryas. The lovely temples and statues in Deogarh, Tala, Udaigiri and Eran come from the Putas, whose empire reached out to the Narmada regions. Chandragupta II maintained an artful residence in Ujjain. The Paramaras were the rulers in Malwa at around the year 1000. The Candella-Rajputs established a state in the north and decorated their capital, Khajuraho, with temples that are among the most beautiful from the Middle Ages in India. In the fourteenth century, the Bundellas took power, which they later yielded from their brilliant capital of Orchha. The Muslims established themselves under the rule of Malwa and made the Mandu fortress into a resplendent capital. A certain general Aurangzeb settled in Bhopal and established an empire state that fired a nineteen round salute during the time of the Raj. The British established a series of independent principalities, which they ran from Nagpur during winter and from Panchmarhi during summer, and brought the rest of the country together under the title of 'Central Provinces' in 1861.

Six million Adivasis belonging to forty different tribes make up part of the predominantly Hindu-speaking population. Their literacy rate is very high at 70 percent. Despite the generally stable political situation, the controversial Narmada weir project resulted in enormous problems for the government as well as for private industry.

This restaurant is advertising *puris*, delicious flat breads that look like balloons after they are fried in oil.

Devout Jainas carved gigantic statues of their saints, the Tirthankaras, from the vertical rock faces at the mountain fortress of Gwalior during the fifteenth century. Barbur, the first mogul emperor, did not like these idol statues and had their faces destroyed.

Orchha was the resplendent capital of
the Bundela-Rajputs in the seventeenth century.
One looks out at the tombstones of the emperors
and the Betwa River through the Raj Mahal.
The Orchha is a charming rustic area nestled
amid imposing and romantic constructions.

The sultan of Mandu and the Bundela-Rajputs took turns ruling Chanderi. The latter had a palace-like temple with places of worship built in various pavilions at the Parameshwar Lake.

Within the city, water is still drawn from deep, round wells with steps.

The beautiful capital of the Chandellas from the tenth to the twelfth centuries is the site of the small town of Khajuraho, now in decay.
The Kandariya Mahadeva is the largest and most beautiful of 25 of the original 85 temples still standing. The walls of the temples are richly
decorated with sculptures: gods and goddesses, lion-like monsters, beautiful girls and couples.

The source of the Namada at Amarkantak is a symbol of purity. Pilgrims and sadhus converge here to bathe. This ascetic rubbed holy ash on his body after washing.

Vishnu was a dwarf-like Brahman in his fifth incarnation, only to grow into a giant who wrested the rule of three worlds away from Bali, the demon king, in three gigantic steps.

The Narmada spills over a rock in Dhandar, roaring through the Haathi ka paon valley.

The great Boramdeo temple in Chattisgarh stands desolate in the wooded mountains. Built in the eleventh century by a not very well-known Ratanpur king, it distinguishes itself with rich decorations, mostly depicting cheerful erotic scenes. The temple terrain is the preferred picnic ground for the girls' schools of Durg, Bhilai and Raipur.

People living in the rural areas of India have no access to modern-day conveniences. Religious festivities, melas and weddings are the highlights of a farmer's year. From time to time, their routine is interrupted by a theater group or acrobats traveling through their area. Even the difficult journey to the weekend market is perceived as a welcome disruption of the day-to-day labor.

290

On the Ramagiri, a hill about 30 miles north of Nagpur, a group of snow white temples attract masses of pilgrims. Rama, Sita and Lakshman supposedly rested here on their way to exile.

A stone idol of a boar is worshipped in a small pavilion in front of the group of temples. It is Vishnu, the savior of the earth, in his third incarnation. This place of worship dates back to the fifth century.

Daily life in Bhopal, capital of Madhya Pradesh.
Traders at the bazaar: the yellowish stones
are chunks of unrefined sugar.
Official porters at the station help travelers
and their luggage to get to their
destinations.
Hanomags: transport resembling a combination
of a rickshaw and a bus.
Musicians wait for clients.

Domes and minarets of three large mosques
compose the skyline of Bhopal. The Moti Masjid
from 1860 had been built in the image of Shah
Jahans's Friday mosque in Delhi, but it does not
have the same dimensions.

The most beautiful Hindu place of worship
stands on a hill in the town of Sanchi.
The beautiful *toranas* (ports), pillars temples
and monastery complexes took centuries
to build. At the northern port of Stupa 1 is a set
of reliefs depicting the temptations put to
Buddha by his wife, Mara, and his daughters.

The smaller Stupa 3, with its relic shrine and the
parasol over it, has only one door decorated
with relief. A sculpture of a snake goddess is in
the foreground.

Trading with old and new goods at the market:
jars that close well and fresh areca nuts.

Raisen is a typical Indian city, with its big street running through the large bazaar, market squares in annexed festival terrains, a bus station and a water reservoir.

Small places of worship – especially for Shiva – are all over the island.

Omkareshwar is another holy place at the Narmada. The Omkareshwar temple with its holy lingam attracts many pilgrims. Travelers visit the area because of its sphere and the bizarre landscape with numerous relics from older temples. The temple is on an island in a stream of the river. It is in the shape of the sign for *Om*. One can travel there with a ferryboat or via a pedestrian bridge.

Gujarat

People in cheerful and vibrant clothing liven up the Rann of Kutch, a meager landscape of parched soil and towns of round clay huts.

Gujarat

The constituent state Gujarat got its definitive shape in 1960 when Bombay was split along the divisional lines of spoken languages. The Gujarati-speaking parts of the country consisted of around two hundred mini-states, made up of the Saurashtra and Kutch empires. Gujarat is very varied geographically: to the northwest, at the border with Pakistan, is the Rann of Kutch, surrounded by fertile fields and salt marshes, and the peninsula of Kutch, which is sometimes transformed into an island during the monsoon season. The Kathiawar peninsula, divided only by the Gulf of Kutch, is sometimes referred to as Saurashtra, "the beautiful land". To the east is the core area of Gujarat over the mainland.

The mainland, with its fertile plains is bordered by wooded parts of the Ghats, the Satpura Mountains, the Vindya Mountains and the Malwa plateau. The single largest cotton area in India spreads out here. Livestock flourish in the northern areas where the monsoons do not have such a drastic impact. Gujarat is one of the three most industrialized constituent states in India. The textile industry in the area is notable. Material from Gujarat became popular in the Arabic world during the thirteenth century. Ahmedabad, the largest city in the area and an industrial, religious and cultural center, became the capital in 1970, when the government moved nearby to the newly established Gandhinagar.

The history of Gujarat began around 2500 BC with the Harappa civilization. More than 100 settlements have been discovered. According to legend, the Yadavas, the clan of India's favorite god Krishna, ruled a

large empire for a thousand years from Dwarka. Around the year zero, the Mauryas ruled over this part of their empire from Junagadh, succeeded by the Ksatrapas and succeeded by the Gupta emperors from the fourth to the sixth centuries. The beautiful temple of Gop dates back to the period. Gurjar tribes from the north established a large empire during the eighth century. (Hence the name of the land.) The beautiful temples of Roda were built during the ninth century. The eleventh and twelfth centuries are nonetheless seen as the Golden Age of Gujarat. The Solanki kings ruled from Patan over a flourishing land.

The unique 'Queens Stepwell' in Patan, a spring with five hundred brilliant statues and numerous Jain temples, was based on the beautiful temples of Modhera and Sejakpur. Financiers and directors of such projects did not only originate from the palaces and the nobles, but from the rich middle class civilians: Jainist merchants, bankers and public officials.

The Islamic era began with raiding, plundering and destruction. Only after the sultanate of Gujarat was established in 1307 and the Moguls started to become prosperous again, did Ahmedabad develop into the beautiful Indian city we know today.

Porbandar Mahatma Gandhi, the father of the Indian nation, was born in 1869. He led India to independence, but could not prevent it from splitting into two states. Currently around ninety percent of the inhabitants of Gujarat are Hindus, 8.5 percent are Muslims and a small percentage belongs to the ever influential Jainas.

Ahmedabad, the capital of Gujarat, is characterized by its Muslim architecture which developed during the heyday of the city under the sultanate of Gujarat and then grew into one of the most beautiful cities in India under the Moguls.
The finely worked stone traceries of the Sidi-Sayyid mosque, with its Tree of Life theme, are the most beautiful of the multitude of the traceries found in this city.

At Sarkhej, outside of the city, various sultans developed an idyllic resort with gardens, an artificial lake, palaces and tombstones around the graves of the holy.

Many of the elderly inhabitants are still illiterate. In order to help them, teachers have taken up positions outside government and court buildings.

The traditional clothing is perfect for the climate and comfortable. The pants, known as *jodhpuris*, are very tight from the ankle to the knee, but they are very roomy above the knee.

308

Extensive ceremonies take place in the main temples in the mornings and the afternoons. The priests keep themselves from accidentally swallowing insects by wearing cloths over their mooths, thus living up to the highest commandment of the Jainas: to protect all forms of life.

The Shatrujaya at Palitana is one of the five holy mountains of the Jainas, which means that it is a very popular pilgrimage destination. Eight hundred and sixty-three temples compete with one another on both mountain tops, as well as in the mountain pass – enclosed by sturdy walls.

311

The 1,939 foot Shatrujaya is scaled via a 2.17 mile system of stairs with three thousand steps. The Jaina nuns nimbly descend the steps.

Junagadh, the original capital of the Rajput state, came under Muslim rule during the fifteenth century. The Nawabs of the Babi dynasty were especially instrumental in determining the oriental romantic image of the city since 1748.

Mount Girnar. This mountain is holy for the Hindus and the Jainas. Hindu sanctuaries are located in the steep hills.

There are resting places along the way for pilgrims who come to visit these holy places and spend four days walking around in the mountain pass, where they are provided with provisions and drink. This dabawallah is delivering milk.

Women from the south of Kathiawar: In addition to colorful outfits and beautiful jewelry, they also have tattoos on their necks.

A group of sixteen beautiful Jain temples, the biggest of which is the Neminath, the twenty-second thirthankara, stand on a plateau under the 3,665 foot western tip of the Ginar.

Along the way to the holy mount of Gimar, there are many opportunities to pay your respects to the gods. Ganesha, a deity with a head of an elephant, is usually very helpful with any human activity – mountain climbing is no exception. Surabhi, the cow that can fulfill any wish, emerged out of the swirling waves of the ocean of milk. Hanuman, the ape god carrying a massive club, is a protective god, just like Bhero, who is much loved and worshipped in Rajasthan and Gujarat and whose temple is guarded by a tiger, the riding animal that is standing on guard by the entrance to the temple of goddess Durga.

In the area north of Bhuj, which is close to the border with Pakistan and is surrounded by – depending on the time of the year, either salt marshes or the deserts of the 'Rann of Kutch', you will find numerous villages scattered over the landscape. The colorful clothing of the villagers is truly amazing. Women wear beautiful jewels and still make their own fluttering skirts, bodices and scarves in the traditional way, each village faithful to its own local customs.

Commemorative stones were erected for brave soldiers who died "heroic deaths." Painted red and decorated with silver foil, colored paper and garlands, they represent idol statuettes for local gods, especially honoring Bhcro.

The maharaja of Wankaner has the right to an eleven round salute. The new palace, built by Amar Sinhji in 1907, was befitting to the magnificence of the empire. It became one of the largest in Gujarat and the Ranjit Vilas palace is widely considered one of the most beautiful in India.

Cracked pillars and weather worn statues only enhance the elegance of the well-proportioned, expertly shaped constructions.

Sixty two miles to the northeast of Ahmedabad is a pastoral environment of temples for Roda, built between the eighth and tenth centuries.

Rajasthan

Pushkar Mela is a religious festival in honor of
Brahma which includes an annual market and
Rajasthan's most important camel markets.

Rajasthan

Rajasthan, the second largest constituent state in India, has a variety of landscapes. Along the 665 mile border with Pakistan, which runs through the Thar Desert, the predominant aspect is that of sand dunes, naked mountain ridges and dry plains that gradually become habitable and fertile field landscapes. To the other side of the Aravalli Range, which runs from the northeast to the southwest, the smaller 'green Rajasthan' with its opulent subtropical vegetation unfolds – thanks to the excessive monsoon rains.

The fame of Rajputana, the land of the 'king's son,' has less to do with its natural beauty than with the Rajputs. Tribes of unknown lineage tried to take power around the seventh century. They subjected themselves as *kshatrias* (warriors) to the caste system, developed a chivalrous code of honor and battled against the empires and against nobles of mighty and less important empires – even far beyond the borders of Rajasthan. Their origins may be the sun, such as the Sisodias of Mewar, or the moon, such as the Bhatis of Jaisalmer, or fire, such as the Solankis, Paramaras or Pratiharas, and only works of art, left in tact through turbulent centuries, remain.

The empires protected their ruling areas with strong fortifications and impressive palaces were built in their capitals, which were subsequently extended by their successors with even larger buildings. They created artificial lakes, wells with steps, temples and tombstones. But traders, especially Jainas, also contributed with their havelis to the unmatched city panoramas. As the empires changed hands, they prof-

ited from the most important trading routes that crossed in Rajputana: from the plains of the Ganges to Sind and from Punjab to Gujarat at the sea.

Muslim armies invaded North India during the eleventh century. The Rajputs lost many battles, but they were not definitively overthrown. The people eventually came to an agreement with the Moguls. Rajput empires led the Muslim armies to spectacular victories. When the Marath pressed into North India during the eighteenth century and the Rajputs started to experience difficulties, they looked for protection from the British and accepted their leadership. After the promise of certain privileges and an abundance of allowances, nineteen empires brought their forces together to form the Republic of India in 1949. Jaipur became the capital of the new constituent state of Rajasthan.

Rajasthan is sparsely populated and underdeveloped. It is a feudal society adjusting very slowly to modern structures where cattle breeding has always been of great importance. The cultivation of sugarcane and cotton is brought about with the irrigation systems of the Indira Gandhi canals. Treasures found below the surface here include lead, zinc and copper as well as gypsum, sandstone, marble and steatite. Only 6 percent of the population works in industry since the majority is mostly involved in generating commodites from the land. Tourism, however, is increasing in importance.

Mount Abu is a mountain mass of the Aravalli
Range. The Jainist Dilwara temples of
the popular 'Hill Station' are historic attractions.
The rich decorations of the pillars and especially
the ceilings of white marble are famously
beautiful.

p.330: The shrine of the Vimala temple from 1031.
p.331: The dome ceiling (bottom left) and of the
shrine (top left/bottom right) of the Vimala temple
and the main dome of the Tejahpala temple
from 1230.

In the dry regions of western Rajasthan, the women's clothes present an unsurpassed display of color– such as here in Pindwara. The men simply wear white. The colorful and refined turbans folded around their heads provide a similar effect.

Kumbhalgarh in the de Aravalli Range is the largest and strongest of the 32 establishments that Maharana Kumbha built in the fifteenth century for the protection of Mewar.
A grandiose panorama unfolds from the palace up to the far off plains in the north.
The great Jain temple of Ranakpur is hidden not far away in the wooded valley. Visitors to the temple decorate this Shiva in its Bhairava form with silver paint and fresh flowers and make the image the focal point of the place of worship amidst luxuriously decorated architecture.

श्री भैरवनाथ (इस्टायकंजी)

One has an incredible view of the 'blue city,' named for the blue painted Brahman houses in the old city, from the Meherangarh fortress atop Jodhpur.
Musicians greet visitors with tympanis and *shenais* at the entrance to the fortress.

Ajmer is a bustling city in the midst of India's most important Muslim sanctuaries. The bazaar provides the inhabitants and pilgrims with the necessary provisions, such as chapattis and delicious bread loaves.
A son reads the newspaper for his father.
Adavasi women fetch wood from outside the city in order to cook.

The Pushkar Mela (the camel festival) is, of course, also about business. Please come in, but take off your shoes first! The drinks are ready. You can bargain as much as you like. But competition plays a role as well – with competitions and prizes determining who has the fastest camel, the most beautiful camel, etc.

Sawai Jai Singh II led Chandra Mahal, had the seven story moon palace built as his residence at the same time the new capital of Jaipur was being built. Parts of it are still inhabited by the royal family.

Monkeys can do anything they like in India. They race over the rooftops of Jaipur in large groups and love to come crashing down on the metal roof sheets of the shops. They make a deafening noise!

A fabric-dyeing family at Gaitor. The colorful rolls of material are given silver ends and then laid out to dry .

Between Jaipur and Amber, the old capital of Kachwaha-Rajputs, is the royal place of commemoration for the deceased Gaitor. Surrounded by a high wall is the marble tombstone of Jai Singh, his family members and successors.

The salon in the palace of Uniara reflects the influence of British rule. The spirit of the time is still present!

The farmers maintain their traditions. It is very difficult for them to be part of modern times.

348

The authenticity of rural Rajasthan is fascinating. An unexpected elephant appears every now and then – such as here between Tonk and Uniara.

Awaiting a monsoon is not an ominous occasion. In the meantime, farmers meet for a chat in the cool alleys of the bazaar of Todaraisingh.

Delhi, Punjab, Himachal Pradesh

Amritsar is the religious center of the Sikhs and the Golden Temple is the most respected sanctuary.
The highest council of the religious community meets in Akhal Takhit, the building with the Golden Dome.

351

Delhi, Punjab, Himachal Pradesh

Delhi did not become the capital of the Republic of India by accident. This city has had a previous run as the capital. According to Mahabharata Indraprashta, the capital of the Pandavas was located here in 1000 BC. The Rajputs ruled over the land for many centuries until 1193 when Qutb-ud-Din took control of the city and demarcated it as his capital by building the Qutub Minar in Dhillika. During the three hundred years that followed, Muslim rulers from various dynasties settled another five capitals within the greater area of the current city, until the grandson of the Mogul Emperor, Akbar Shahjahanabad, established the current Old Delhi with the Red Fort and the Great Mosque.

The British began assembling New Delhi as a Capitol in 1911 and declared it the official capital of British India in 1931. The contrasts between the royal measurements of the city, with the representative governing center, and the bazaar life at the Chandi Chowk, as well as between the modern city and the imposing relics encompassed in its great past, make Delhi very attractive. Delhi is an independent 'Union Territory' set within the border areas of the constituent states of Haryana and Uttar Pradesh.

Punjab, the land of five streams, was the heart of the cultural landscape and granary of early India from the third millennium BC. It is the native land of Hindus, Muslims and Sikhs. The land was divided in 1947. Panic stricken refugees fled the bloodbaths (perpetrated by both sides) en masse. About two million Sikhs alone fled from Pakistan to India.

The Sikhs, whose religion dates back to Guru Nanak, who preached peaceful coexistence between Hinduism and Muslims around 1600, lived in an egalitarian, casteless society. They venerated only one god with no concrete shape. Their fiery desire for autonomy led to the new division of the Indian state of Punjab in 1966; the mountainous landscape to the northeast became Himachal Pradesh and the southern part of the country became the new constituent state. The new Punjab constituent state is located along the Sutlej and Beas, tributaries of the Indus, where the Amritsar religious center is also located, with the Sikhs forming a 55 percent majority. The city of Chandigarh was built with the birth of Haryana as the capital. Punjab produces a quarter of the grain and one third of the milk produced in India. Industry is busy expanding. The income per capita is double that of the Indian average: this is the argument of the advocates for an independent Sikh state of Khalistan.

Himachal Pradesh was established in 1948 with the fusion of thirty independent 'Punjab Hill States' and it got its definitive borders in 1966 when the districts of Kulu, Kangra and Lahaul-Spiti were added. This constituent state has a great landscape and cultural beauty. It stretches from the North Indian low-lying plains through the Shivalik Mountains up to the 20,000 feet high mountains in the High Himalayas. The rich culture of Buddhist monasteries and Hindu temples made from wood and pearl stone in the deep ravines have been preserved. The slopes are covered with 40 percent forest. Agriculture and fruit cultivation are the most prominent economic activities. The red apples from Himachal Pradesh are sold all over India. The capital of Simla, at a height of 7,200 feet, sheltered the British when it became too dangerous for them in Delhi.

In the twelfth century Qutb-ud-Din Aibak had
the Quwwat-ul-Islam mosque built and the Qutb
Minar became the first Muslim Empire on Indian
soil. Delhi is the undisputed capital of India – for
the seventh time.

The tombstone for Humayun, the second Mogul
Emperor, represented the last Muslim dynasty
ruling India from New Delhi.
The temple of the Bahais was used as the
model for modern India: he made a call for
freedom, tolerance and an open attitude
towards the world..

Daily life takes place on the streets in modern-day New Delhi. 'Shops' are opened wherever space can be found. All sorts of articles and services are sold, ranging from palm reading to hand decoration. An ointment of henna is used to make the patterns and they fade after a few days.

The shopping streets teem during lunchtime. White collar workers jostle for a space in fast-food restaurants.

Connaught Place was designed by the British as the trade center of the capital. It consists of a double ring of buildings enclosing a large square. The highways run in a radial pattern in all directions.

Unique chic businesses, souvenir shops, expensive restaurants and snack bars are situated under shadowy arches.

Chandigarh, the capital of Punjab and Haryana, was designed by Le Corbusier as a living organism. He designed the 'head' himself: the parliament building, the ministries and the Supreme Court. The 'Open Hand Monument' – forty two feet high, weighing 45 tons and mobile as a weather vane, it is the national and municipal symbol of harmony and peace.

The 'Rock Garden' offers a relaxing contrast to the concrete rationality and stress of the city. The artist, Nek Chand, tried to play with visitors' perspectives and entertain them with a variety of imaginative creations.

A former road construction supervisor created an artful adventure park with mazes, surprising viewpoints and innumerable groups of figures, out of industrial waste and trash on 24 acres of jungle.

The Golden Temple in Amritsar is in the middle
of a square pool, filled with the nectar of
immortality, *amrita*. Ranjit Singh had
the building covered with gilded copper
plates in 1802, which gave the temple its
name.

One of the five commandments Sikhs must
obey is to carry a knife with an iron handle.
Today it is usually a small knife on the turban
which keeps the folded hair together.

Jammu, the former winter residence of the maharajas of Kashmir, has retained little of its former glory. Judicial authorities are now hosted in their palaces. Lawyers provide their clients with advice on tables in front of them.

Temples such as the Ranbireshvar complex must nowadays be protected by the police because the danger of terrorism is lurking everywhere.

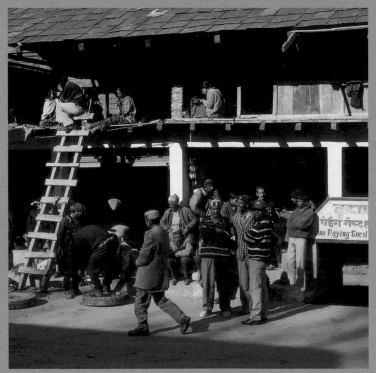

The large bronze idol and the carvings at the Lakshnadevi temple are very striking.

Brahmaur at the top end of the Ravi River became the capital of the state of Chamba in the ninth century. Some of the picturesque temples that occupy the square and tower above the city date back to the seventh century.

The heavy clothes of the women in the Kullu valley with the characteristic checkered patterns are indicative of the rough climate of these regions.

The mountain towns on the eastern side of the Beas Valley, between Nagar and Kullu, have maintained their Asian influences. The roofs of the typical wooden houses are often covered with authentic tiles.

Ladakh

The miracle play is opened in the Lamayuru monastery. Lamas walk around the festival terrain and blow on their *ragdun* – long copper horns.

Ladakh

Ladakh forms a part of the constituent state with Jammu and Kashmir. Each of the three country parts has its own, unmistakable identity; Jammu is predominantly Hindu; Kashmir is Islamic and Ladakh is a stronghold of Tibetan Buddhism. Ladakh was conqured in 1834 by the Dogra-Rajputs from Jammu. Gulap Singh also took reign over Kashmir from the Sikhs in 1846. The British acknowledged the area of power of the Hindu maharaja and the last successor opted to be a part of India in 1947 – the start of the Kashmir conflict.

Bordered by the Karakorum Range to the north and the High Himalaya in the south, Ladakh is an enormous desert in the high mountains which permits very harsh living conditions. People living along the Indus and its tributaries at a height of 11,500 feet developed a unique culture through the centuries on the basis of Buddhism. The first kingdom was established in the ninth century. Ladakh became a very important arbitrator between the Buddhist Kashmir and Tibet. The sixteenth century is seen as the Golden Age of Ladakh, but despair set in during the seventeenth century with defeat at the hands of the Mogul forces: obligatory payments were to be made, there was religious suppression and further weakening by tribal disagreements.

The rain clouds of the monsoons do not reach Ladakh very often. Streams and rivers are fed by melting water from glaciers. Green oases were established around towns by directing water and hard work. The vegetation period is very short, however. The soil is frozen solid for eight months of the year. Mostly barley is cultivated here, the most

basic food type is consumed as tsjampa (roasted flour) or as tsjang (barley beer). Wheat, potatoes and various vegetables, apricots and walnut trees grow in favorable zones. This is not possible at greater heights, however. Sheep, goats and, to a lesser extent, yaks, produce wool, milk and butter — the main ingredients of the most important food from Ladakh: butter tea.

The Ladakhis are peaceful and friendly. They are devout Buddhists. Their religious customs are present everywhere. Groups of stupas and prayer flags flap merrily in the wind and liven up the harsh landscape. Long mani walls made from stone with prayers enclosed in them line the paths to the innumerable monasteries, the solid and picturesque rocks and the slopes along river valleys.

The monks take care of the people and their religious and psychological needs. They lead them with ceremonies and rituals. Monastery festivals are annual highlights in Ladakh. Laymen, farmers and townsfolk eagerly provide for the earthly needs of monks as compensation.

Leh, the capital of Ladakh, is located at the foot of the old king's castle at the end of a tributary of the Indus. The atmosphere of this city is rapidly changing. Countless numbers of hotels and guest houses offer visitors to Ladakh a welcome place to stay. The Ladahakis are very concerned about the increasing influence of Islam from Kashmir, fearing that they may lose their Buddhist identity.

Typical head covers in Ladakh are the cylindrical *tibi*. They are worn by women and men.

Due to the instability in the Kashmir Valley, the 301 mile road between Manali and Leh is the best alternative to reach Ladakh over land. The highest mountain connection in the world stretches over four maintain passes where weather circumstances can cause time-consuming delays – as can be seen here at the 16,086 foot Baralache pass.

Musicians lead the dances at this miracle play with long horns, drums and cymbals.

Padmasambhava with their metal masks perform as the beautifully dressed heroes (top left), led by dancers without masks (bottom right). The *atsharas* with their funny masks depict Hindu priests. They pretend to be idiotic. The highlight of the tsjam dances approaches with the performance of Yama, the god of death, also known as Dharmaraja, king of the religious laws (top right). In one dramatic scene, he crushes a small human figure made of bread dough with his sword and symbolically defeats evil in this way.

Visitors to the plays, such as these two Dogpa women from Westladakh and the distinguished lady with her heavy *perak*, allow themselves to be carried away by events in the courtyard of the monastery. The dances are festival highlights of the year – for monks as well as laymen.

Prayer flags flutter in the wind. A lovely sight at Leh with the king's bridge and the 16,500 foot high mountains of the Ladakhketen in the background.

Shey, the holy book from the monastery, is carried over a great stupa field in a procession and then returned. The books in this case are stacks of manuscript skins, clamped between two wooden book plates and folded in a cloth.

The valley of the Indus is a desert away from the irrigated fields: sand dunes, decayed stupas and poplars.
In addition to the 26 foot high statue of Buddha, there are also lovely murals that demand attention in the Shakyamuni temple of Shey.
They display the great holy of the Kargyüpa sect such as Naropa, the great Indian *mahasiddhi*.

The Nubra valley is located to the North of Leh, on the other side of the 18,392 feet high mountain pass. Sumur is one of the most important monasteries of the region.

The inhabitants of the surrounding towns patiently await the ceremony following the arrival of a highly placed lama to the outer monastery court.

The Alchi monastery, built in the eleventh century, maintains the high artistic standards of those days. The beautiful and original portal of the meeting hall was shaped like the stone Hindu temples from the period. The stupas at the entrance are decorated, just as the temples, with precious paintings. They depict Padmasambhava with other holies or, such as shown here, with the 'learning' position of the hands.

Miracle plays in the Lamayuru monastery; the spectators on the roof are of the highest rank.

One of the ten dreaded gods of Hindu and Old Tibetan origin who was suppressed by Padmasambhava.

The Likir monastery stands at one end of a desolate slope of the valley of the Indus. Numerous stupas surround the *gompa* (monastery).

A steep, twenty-three foot rock in the border area between the Islamic and Buddhist Ladakh into which a sculpture of the Maitreya, the Buddha of the future, was half carved. The sculpture was most probably made around the eighth century by artists from Kashmir and is seen as indicative of the direction of development in Ladakh.

Index